a taste of
PROVIDENCE

*A guide to 14 of Providence's finest restaurants,
plus a cookbook of their most popular recipes.*

by Gillian Drake and Terrence Gavan

PINEAPPLE PUBLICATIONS • NEWPORT, RHODE ISLAND

Books in the "Taste of . . ." series:

A TASTE OF PROVIDENCE
A TASTE OF NEWPORT
A TASTE OF CAPE COD
A TASTE OF PROVINCETOWN

order coupon on page 87

"A Taste of Providence"
compiled by Gillian Drake & Terrence Gavan

Written by Terrence Gavan

Designed and produced by Gillian Drake

Printed by Shank Painter Printing Co. Inc., Provincetown, Mass.   ISBN 0-929249-02-X

INTRODUCTION

The Providence renaissance is in full swing. The city, which has experienced decades of decay, was once one of America's industrial and cultural giants. Now, as Providence rediscovers its lost identity and rich cultural heritage, it's forging a new personality as a center for the arts and as a regional commercial powerhouse. Led by such institutions as Brown University, the Rhode Island School of Design and Johnson and Wales, Providence has developed a solid reputation for education and culture.

While much of Providence has been preserved, particularly in the historic east side, architectural gems are continually uncovered in neighborhoods throughout the city. And Providence boasts some of America's best architectural examples of the Colonial and Victorian eras. Ambitious development projects are revitalizing the once moribund central city, and the arts are flourishing in newly renovated downtown theaters. All of this promises to restore the city to much of its 18th and 19th century prominence, albeit with a contemporary slant.

Providence restaurants are right in the thick of this renaissance movement. The city's restaurant scene is vibrant and spirited, serving some of the best American and European cuisine. Most of Providence's fine restaurants are fairly new, having risen with this renaissance. You'll find them interesting and innovative— menu, ambiance, proprietors— with remarkable diversity.

There's something for every palate and penchant. This can be seen in the elegant and authentic French dining of **La France, Pot au Feu** and **Rue de l'Espoir**; the contemporary leading-edge decor and cuisine of **Adesso** and **In Prov**; the myriad seafood of **J. Wales, Hemenways** and **Down Under II**; the regional Italian fare and upbeat ambiance of **Raphael's**; the classic elegance and lavishness of **Audrey's** and the **Arboretum Restaurant**; and the historic romance of Victorian **Angels** and colonial **Nathaniel Porter Inn**.

Welcome to Providence. Please sit down and enjoy yourself.

CONTENTS

DOWNTOWN PROVIDENCE

1. POT AU FEU • 44 Custom House St., Providence • (401) 273-8953
SUNDAY BRUNCH / LUNCH / DINNER

2. ADESSO • 161 Cushing Street, Providence • (401) 521-0770
LUNCH / DINNER

3. HEMENWAY'S • One Old Stone Square, South Main Street, Providence
(401) 351-8570 • LUNCH / DINNER / BAR

4. RUE DE L'ESPOIR • 99 Hope St., Providence • (401) 751-8890
BRUNCH / LUNCH / DINNER / BAR

5. IN PROV • 50 Kennedy Plaza, Providence • (401) 351-8770
TAKE-OUT BREAKFAST / LUNCH / DINNER / LATE SUPPER / BAR

6. LA FRANCE • 960 Hope St., Providence • (401) 331-9233
LUNCH / DINNER

7. RAPHAEL'S • 207 Pine Street, Providence • (401) 421-4646
LUNCH / DINNER / LOUNGE / COURTYARD

8. ANGELS • 125 North Main Street, Providence • (401) 273-0310
DINNER / BAR

9. PASTICHE • 92 Spruce Street, Providence
(401) 861-5190
DESSERT & COFFEE

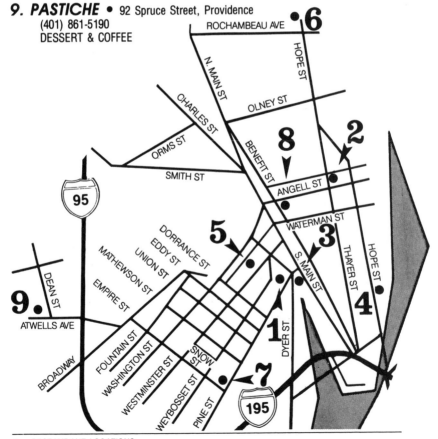

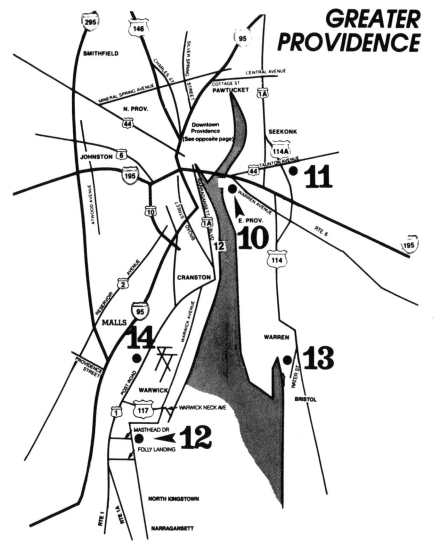

GREATER PROVIDENCE

10. *ARBORETUM RESTAURANT*
39 Warren Ave., East Providence • (401) 438-3686 • LUNCH / DINNER / BAR

11. *AUDREY'S* • Routes 114A & 44, Seekonk, Mass. • (508) 336-4636
BREAKFAST / BRUNCH / LUNCH / DINNER

12. *DOWN UNDER II* • 1 Masthead Drive, Warwick • (401) 885-6400
DINNER / BAR

13. *NATHANIEL PORTER INN* • 125 Water St., Warren • (401) 245-6622
LUNCH / AFTERNOON TEA / DINNER

14. *J. WALES*
2099 Post Road, Warwick • (401) 732-3663; SEA-FOOD • LUNCH / DINNER

POT AU FEU

You'll be greeted with "Bon jour, Pot au Feu!" when you call for reservations. This greeting is a fitting precursor to a French adventure you're not likely to forget.

Located in Providence's small but bustling financial district, **Pot au Feu** is tucked away on short Customs House Street, just a few blocks from Kennedy Plaza. The historic facade of this 1875 building contains huge plate glass windows framed by ornate cast iron columns. Look for the distinctive pink and black Pot au Feu sign.

The irrepressible owners, Bob and Ann Burke, took over Pot au Feu in 1986. Ann traces her meteoric career in the Providence restaurant business back to 1981, when she began as a waitress at Pot au Feu. She quickly rose to manager, and by 1986 she owned the restaurant. Now, with husband Bob, a human dynamo and former insurance adjuster, and a triad of talented chefs she runs Pot au Feu with a driving sense of perfection and a relentless will to innovate.

Pot au Feu consists of two distinct dining areas separated by a flight of stairs. Downstairs, the Bistro is a cozy and casual hideaway with brick floors, stone walls and beamed ceilings. The Bistro offers a lighter (but nevertheless substantial) fare consisting of French regional entrees, omelets, quiches, crepes, soups and salads. As you might expect, the Bistro serves a highly acclaimed French onion soup, hearty and enriched with white wine. The Bistro also serves a dish called Pot au Feu, a traditional French stew of beef and chicken braised with a mixture of fresh vegetables. Note the unique Parisian-style zinc bar and the authentic map of the Paris metro system on the wall.

Upstairs, the Salon is the epitome of Gallic elegance and romance. Crisp white linen, fresh flowers and candlelight complement the soothing pink and grey motif. Many of the tables overlook the street through the broad plate-glass windows. If you can get it, ask for Bob Burke's favorite table which has a good view of the outside but is also centrally situated for enjoying the elegant interior.

Pot au Feu unabashedly celebrates French culture by staging a series of special culinary events each year. The *Fete du Printemps,* held in April and May, is a rite of spring and each week features the food and wines of eight different regions of France. Every fall, the *Fete de la Vendange* celebrates the wine harvest with a tour and wine tasting at Sakonnet Vineyards in Little Compton. The day-long event includes a picnic at the vineyards and culminates with an eight-course dinner at the Salon. These events are the creation of Bob Burke, who is a vigorous promoter and marketeer of the restaurant and French culture.

The Salon offers five course *prix fixe* (fixed price) dining as well as *a la carte* selections. The *prix fixe* menu covers all entrees and includes appetizer, soup, salad and dessert. These portions are smaller, so even with a modest appetite you can enjoy all five courses at a reasonable cost. The Salon menu is extensive and elaborate. If any one category dominates it's probably seafood. The menu covers practically the entire range and includes salmon, scallops, sole, swordfish, monkfish, and shrimp. Each entree is usually prepared two different ways (poached and either roasted or sauteed) and served with an innovative melange of herbs, spices and wine.

House specialties include three different duck entrees—one is sauteed boneless breast served in classic *confit* style with duck leg and a sauce of red wine, peppercorns and duck fume. Fresh Norwegian salmon is another favorite—you can order it poached with white wine, fish fume, cream and shallots, or pan-roasted with a strawberry *meuniere* sauce.

The Pot au Feu produces award-winning desserts on a regular basis. Judges at the annual Trinity Dessert Social have declared the Vanilla Mousse (light, creamy with praline sauce) the absolute best of the day (recipe follows), and the Chocolate Torte the "most decadent." Also, *Food and Wine* magazine featured the Pumpkin Cheesecake.

The wine list offers a lengthy selection of French and American wines. The house wines are Moreau Blanc (Burgundy) and Valbon Rouge. There are numerous wines available by the glass, and an impressive array of cognacs, brandies and cordials.

When discussing Pot au Feu's mission, Bob Burke says, "We are trying to create an authentic dining experience that is the equal of the great restaurants and bistros of France, and by operating with style we want to excite our customers and ourselves as well."

"Bon jour, Pot au Feu."

POT AU FEU
"Paris in Providence"
44 Custom House Street, Providence • (401) 273-8953

OPEN: 7 days a week, Sept. to May
       June, July and August, closed Sun.
SUNDAY BRUNCH: 12:00 to 4:00
LUNCH: 11:30 to 3:00 in the Bistro
          11:30 to 2:00 in the Salon
DINNER: from 5:00 in the Bistro, from 6:00 in the Salon
SEATS: Bistro: 50, Salon: 55
CHILDREN'S PORTIONS: not available
CREDIT CARDS: AMEX, DC, MC, VISA
PARKING: in public parking lots nearby
RESERVATIONS: advised in the Salon; not accepted in the Bistro

Choucroute Garnie

SERVES 6-8

6 knockwurst sausages
12 small bratwurst sausages
6 bockwurst sausages
6 pork chops
2 lb. sauerkraut, drained
1 medium onion, diced
½ lb. bacon, chopped
½ cup veal or chicken stock
½ cup white wine
4 to 6 juniper berries
3 bay leaves
½ teaspoon thyme
½ teaspoon caraway seeds
12 small Bliss potatoes
black pepper to taste

Sauerkraut: cook bacon, add diced onions and saute in bacon fat until tender. Add drained sauerkraut, seasonings, stock and wine. Remove from heat, stir, and place in covered casserole. Bake in oven at 375 degrees for one hour.

Parboil potatoes with skins on and set aside to keep warm. Lightly grill chops and sausages. Combine potato, sausages and chops with sauerkraut. Bake for half an hour until done.

Remove and arrange on a platter. Garnish with parsley. Serve with Dijon mustard.

Filet of Salmon & Seafood Sausages with Beurre Blanc SERVES 8

2 lb. Norwegian salmon filet
2 cups court bouillon
16 boudins de fruit de mer (see following recipe)

Beurre Blanc aux Framboises:
3 oz. heavy cream
2 tablespoons shallots, minced
½ pint raspberries
8 oz. butter
juice of half a lemon
1 cup red wine

Beurre Blanc a l'Orange:
3 oz. heavy cream
2 teaspoons shallots, minced
juice and zest of half an orange
1 oz. Grand Marnier
8 oz. butter
juice of half a lemon
1 cup white wine

To make the Beurre Blanc aux Framboises: combine shallots, red wine, lemon juice and cream in a saucepan. Puree and strain raspberries and add to mixture. Reduce by ⅔ over medium heat. Lower heat and whisk in small pieces of butter until sauce is smooth. Reserve in a warm place.

To make the Beurre Blanc a l'Orange: combine shallots, white wine, lemon juice, orange juice, Grand Marnier, orange zest and cream in a saucepan. Reduce by ⅔ over medium heat. Lower heat and whisk in small pieces of butter until sauce is smooth. Reserve in a warm place.

Final preparation: Cut salmon into 4 oz. portions. Poach salmon and sausages in court bouillon. When cooked remove salmon from pan and sauce with beurre blanc aux framboises. Garnish with fresh raspberries. Remove sausages from pan and sauce with beurre blanc a l'orange. Garnish with fresh parsley and serve immediately.

Boudins de Fruits du Mer
Seafood Sausages

1 lb. sole
1 lb. scallops
½ lb. salmon
½ lb. lobster meat, cooked
1½ cups heavy cream
1 teaspoon salt
1 teaspoon tarragon, chopped
1 teaspoon chives, chopped
1 teaspoon parsley or chervil, chopped
cayenne pepper to taste
sausage casings

Shell lobster and remove meat. Bone and skin fish. Remove muscle from scallops. Cut fish into strips ½" wide. Grind lobster, scallops, salmon and sole using a hand grinder or grinding attachment on a food processor. Mix the ground seafood with seasonings and herbs and ½ cup of the cream. Whip the remaining cream and fold into the mixture. Stuff into casings and twist into individual sausages. Let set for several hours in a refrigerator. Heat by poaching in a light fish stock and serve with sauce.

Confit de Canard Bigarade

2 ducks, 4 to 5 lbs. each
1 cup rock salt
5 lbs. duck fat
sauce Bigarade (see following recipe)

Split ducks in half along breast plate. Remove backbone. Remove wings at joints. Separate legs from breast. Remove excess fat and skin. Render duck in a heavy casserole or skillet over low heat until skin becomes crisp. Remove from heat and rub ducks with salt. Set aside in refrigerator for 24 hours. Wipe off salt. Heat duck fat (vegetable oil may be added to cover ducks) in heavy casserole and simmer duck for 1½ hours. If desired, the fat my be seasoned with clove, mace and bay leaves. To preserve and store, place duck tightly in a container and cover with strained duck fat. The duck may be kept for several months preserved in this manner. When ready to serve, saute the duck lightly to remove excess fat and then roast in the oven at 350 degrees for 5 to 10 minutes to heat through. Serve with sauce Bigarade.

Mousse de Poisson

2 lbs. sole
1 lb. onion, chopped
3 oz. butter
1 cup white wine
3 cups clam stock
2 tablespoons lemon juice
4 tablespoons gelatin
1 cup water
1 cup mayonnaise
1 tablespoons chives, chopped
10 oz. cream cheese
3 cups heavy cream, whipped
2 teaspoons horseradish sauce
1 cup sour cream
16 oz. Nova Scotia smoked salmon

Saute onions in butter. Add fish, wine, 1 cup clam stock and lemon juice. Cover and poach until fish flakes, about 3 to 5 minutes. Strain and cool fish.

Soften gelatin in 1 cup water. Add this to 2 cups hot clam stock and cook to dissolve the gelatin completely. Cool until mixture is syrupy.

Puree fish, cream cheese, horseradish, and gelatin mixture. Stir into the whipped cream. Add mayonnaise, sour cream and chives. Stir. Assemble in two terrine pans in layers, first a layer of smoked salmon, then a layer of mousse, covered by another layer of smoked salmon and then mousse, and topped with a layer of over-lapping slices of smoked salmon. Chill and serve in slices. Makes two loaves, 12 portions each loaf.

Croque Madame

2 slices bread
2 oz. turkey breast, sliced thin
2 oz. Swiss cheese, sliced thin
1 tablespoon mustard butter
quiche custard

Spread slices of bread with mustard butter. Assemble turkey and cheese on bread. Dip in quiche custard (eggs beaten with milk). Saute on grill until golden and cheese has melted.

Creme Celeste

3 to 4 tablespoons gelatin
⅓ cup water, approximately
1 pint heavy cream
7/8 cup sugar
1 pint sour cream
¼ cup Brandy (Bardinet or Gaston de la Grange)
1½ cups strawberries (frozen sweetened slices)
1½ cups raspberries (frozen sweetened slices)

Dissolve gelatin in cold water. It should look like applesauce in consistency. Completely dissolve sugar in cream over heat in a three-quart pan. Add softened gelatin to cream and sugar and stir over low heat until gelatin is completely dissolved. (No clear specks should be visible on the back of a wooden spoon.) Heat until almost boiling and take off heat.

Add sour cream to cream mixture and incorporate with a whip. Add brandy and stir, being careful not to create too many air bubbles.

Pour mixture into a shallow pan, cover with plastic wrap and refrigerate. Serve in 5 oz. champagne glasses with pureed strawberry/raspberry sauce.

Vanilla Mousse

2 eggs, separated
1 pint heavy cream
1 vanilla bean, split
¾ cup sugar

half tablespoon gelatin
1 tablespoon water,
  for softening gelatin
½ tablespoon vanilla extract

Soften gelatin in a tablespoon of water. Place 1 cup of cream, ¼ cup of sugar and the vanilla bean in a saucepan and bring to a boil. In a bowl, whisk yolks until fluffy and lemony in color. Add hot cream to yolks very slowly, whisking all the while. Add softened gelatin to mixture. Return mixture to heat briefly to completely dissolve gelatin. Strain mixture into another container, scrape vanilla bean and add to custard and chill.

In a separate chilled bowl, whip the remaining cream with vanilla extract. When custard is cool enough, whip slightly to smooth it out and fold in heavy cream. Return to refrigerator.

In a clean bowl and with a clean whisk, whip up egg whites, adding remaining sugar slowly after the whites come to a soft peak. Fold mousse mixture gently but thoroughly into egg whites, let set up briefly in refrigerator and pipe into serving glasses. Top with praline sauce when ready to serve.

ADESSO

A California cafe in Rhode Island? That's right, you'll find **Adesso** in the College Hill section of Providence's east side. The word adesso means "now" in Italian, but the restaurant is more contemporary American than Italian. Billing itself as a California cafe on the leading edge of American cusine, Adesso has a novel menu, at least for Rhode Island. But Adesso is more than just a pretty menu. It's a unique, unpretentious cafe with an informal manner, strong in Italian influence but steeped in American style. Since the restaurant is located in the upscale residential east side, it draws a clientele ranging from local residents to Brown University students and faculty.

In 1986, after studying trends and visiting California restaurants, the owners opened Adesso. They concluded that Providence needed an informal but quality American-style restaurant. "We noticed the great popularity in California of the stylish but unpretentious restaurant — no airs, not stuffy, just unique American appeal," they explained.

The interior is decidedly high-tech — silver table cloths, track lighting and skylights — softened by a color scheme of pink and grey. The black planetarium-like ceiling is dotted with tiny spotlights, and neon fixtures adorn the walls.

The expansive menu consists of pastas, pizzas, and mesquite-grilled entrees. A long marble-bound cooking area houses a productive mesquite grill and a fascinating wood-fueled pizza oven. The grill is used for cooking all sorts of entrees: chicken (stuffed with pesto), pork chops (glazed with red pepper jelly), scallops (with a Mandarin-orange cream sauce), tuna (with tomato-mint salsa and cucumber noodles), swordfish (with pineapple-carambola sauce), and veal chops (with wild mushrooms and shallots). You can even get a grilled warm duck salad with radicchio, mushrooms, grapefruit, orange, Grand Marnier and walnut oil.

The imaginative pasta dishes range from black pepper linquine with shrimp, asparagus and sun-dried tomato in a vodka, butter and cream sauce, to fettuccine with lobster meat, butter, sage and parmigiano cheese.

The pizzas are truly epicurean. One ten-inch size fits all, but there are twelve eccentric styles to choose from. Try barbequed chicken with cilantro, red onion, smoked gouda, and mozzarella; or lamb sausage with roasted red and yellow peppers, wild mushrooms and a Madeira-mustard sauce; or asparagus with pancetta, onion, mozzarella, fontina and mascarpone cheeses. You'll also find calzone stuffed with ricotta, parmigiano, mozzarella, sauteed spinach, garlic and wild mushrooms. The imposing pizza oven is a wonderful contraption. They put the wood right in the oven with the pizza (at a discreet distance, of course), and the burning wood rapidly heats the oven stone to a very high temperature.

At Adesso, much thought goes into presentation. Check out the endive and apple salad arrayed in pinwheels on a stark black plate and adorned with hand-chopped red peppers, watercress, blue cheese and walnuts. Or if you're an Italian patriot, try the arugula, radicchio and endive salad; it's presented in the colors of the Italian flag.

Adesso's most popular dessert, Tirami Su (loosely translated as "pick me up"), is a sort of cake made with Italian lady fingers, espresso, Myer's rum, mascarpone cheese and dusted with Dutch chocolate.

Extraordinary attention to detail, an unusual menu utilizing the freshest ingredients, and an enthusiastic waitstaff are Adesso's cornerstones. The exhaustive research by the owners seems to have paid off.

ADESSO
A Chic California Cafe
161 CUSHING STREET, PROVIDENCE • (401) 521-0770

LUNCH: Mon.-Sat. 11:45-2:30
DINNER: Mon.-Thurs. 5:00-10:30, Fri. & Sat. 5-midnight, Sun. 4:30-10:30
SEATS: 112
CREDIT CARDS: AMEX, MC, VISA
PARKING: private lot
RESERVATIONS: no reservations taken

Papardelle with Wild Mushrooms

SERVES 2

2 oz. 100% olive oil
2 cloves garlic, sliced
1 cup domestic mushrooms
1 cup shitake mushrooms
½ cup Marsala wine
2 oz. veal stock
1 sundried tomato, julienned
1 tablespoon diced tomato
1 oz. butter
1 oz. Parmigiano cheese, grated
2 portions cooked papardelle pasta
chopped parsley for garnish

Heat the olive oil in a pan and saute the garlic and mushrooms. Deglaze the pan with the Marsala and veal stock. Add the diced tomato, sundried tomato and butter and saute quickly over high heat. Add the freshly cooked papardelle and toss in the pan with Parmigiano cheese. Served in warmed pasta bowls garnished with chopped parsley.

Adesso Eggplant Pizza

SERVES 2

your favorite pizza dough
2 tablespoons seasoned tomato sauce
½ teaspoon chopped garlic
½ teaspoon oregano
4 oz. whole-milk Mozzarella cheese, grated
1 cup sliced sauteed eggplant, ¼" thick
½ cup fresh tomato, chopped
2 tablespoons fresh basil, chopped
a few red onion rings
Parmigiano cheese

Stretch the pizza dough to the desired size and place on a cookie sheet. Spread with tomato sauce, garlic, oregano, Mozzarella cheese and eggplant. Sprinkle with fresh tomato, basil, onion rings, Parmigiano cheese and a little more Mozzarella. Bake in a preheated oven at 500 degrees for about 10 minutes. Sprinkle with fresh chopped basil before serving.

Adesso Tirami Su

2 cups cooled espresso
1 oz. rum or brandy or Amaretto
4 egg whites, beaten stiff
4 egg yolks
½ cup sugar
12 oz. Mascarpone cheese
48 Italian lady fingers
2 tablespoons powdered Dutch chocolate

Make a pastry cream by beating together the egg yolks and sugar. Blend in beaten egg whites, then the Mascarpone cheese. Chill. Meanwhile, combine the espresso and liquor.

Assemble the Tirami Su in this manner on a serving plate: dip the lady fingers in the espresso/liquor mix and form one layer on the serving plate. Carefully cover with a layer of the chilled cheese mixture. Repeat with a layer of lady fingers, and with another layer of cheese mixture. Repeat with a third layer. Refrigerate until it is well chilled. Just before serving, dust with the powdered chocolate. Cut into squares, or simply serve out portions with a large serving spoon.

AUDREY'S

Audrey's is the training facility for Johnson and Wales University, the premier culinary arts school in America. Johnson and Wales alumni are famous throughout the world for their culinary skills and list among their number a virtual "who's who" of American chefs.

Audrey's is located in the Johnson and Wales Inn, just outside Providence. The inn first opened in 1985, and has undergone extensive renovations. The elegant lobby won the Designer's Circle Award from *Lodging Hospitality* magazine for the best renovation of 1988. This luxurious lobby leads into the similarly-designed Audrey's restaurant.

The restaurant interior has a comfortable English club look with an abundance of rich mahogany and brass. The spacious dining room is well endowed with attractive sporting prints and large stuffed arm chairs. There's an expansive bar and a dance floor on one side. Plush carpeting and subdued lighting complete the decor and create an atmosphere that's comfortable but romantic.

The restaurant becomes a beehive of activity when the tuxedoed staff goes about its business filling water glasses, issuing bread, serving salad, and taking orders. The operation of Audrey's is serious business, and it's a delight watching the students and teachers in action. It's all very subtle and unobtrusive, unless you happen to be looking for it.

The menu is seasonal, so it changes four times a year, but there's a weekly menu of special dishes for added variety featuring hearty New England cuisine and continental favorites. Executive chef Andy Lussier, a Johnson and Wales graduate, supervises Audrey's kitchen. Andy is renowned for his regional dishes such as quail served in peppercorn pastry or grilled venison with wholewheat fettuccine.

Game dishes are popular at Audrey's, even with the appetizers. You can get pheasant pate with wild mushrooms or ragout of game—rabbit and venison in a red wine sauce served in a puff pastry shell.

Seasonal entrees that you might find include Field & Stream—a fillet of Coho salmon stuffed with crayfish and herbs, accompanied by a roasted quail set in a potato nest. Or you may encounter the Veal Pommery—cutlets sauteed in butter and served with a light-grained mustard cream sauce and garnished with wild mushrooms. Another possibility is Escallops of Haddock with Prosciutto—fillets dipped in a light egg batter and sauteed with cured ham and fresh basil, garnished with red peppers and peas.

More traditional fare is also available. Try the Veal Oscar, topped with asparagus, crabmeat and hollandaise sauce, or the Baked Stuffed Pork Chop, stuffed with a flavorful dressing, braised, and served with a rich Madeira sauce.

The future leaders of the hospitality industry are being trained here, so all ingredients are fresh and of the highest quality, and all food is prepared on the premises. This includes the pastas, breads, rolls, pastries, ice cream and sherbet. The constantly changing selection of dishes includes a light entree containing no salt, cream or fat for those on restricted diets.

The Johnson and Wales Inn is a first-class hotel with deluxe rooms and suites, all decorated in the classic English style. Like Audrey's, the hotel is staffed by the University's hospitality students.

Audrey's is a relaxing experience, but it's also a romantic and elegant one, definitely designed to impress your date.

AUDREY'S

Fine Regional Cuisine and Hearty New England Fare
ROUTES 114A & 44, SEEKONK, MASS. • (508) 336-4636

BREAKFAST: 6:30-10
BRUNCH: 10:30-2:30
LUNCH: 11:30-2:30, except Sun.
DINNER: 5:00-10:00, Sat. 6-11:00
BAR: Audrey's Lounge, noon to midnight every day
CREDIT CARDS: AMEX, CB, DC, MC, VISA
PARKING: ample free parking
RESERVATIONS: advised

Forager's Reward Salad

SERVES 6

1 lb. fiddleheads (in season, optional)
1 lb. chanterelle mushrooms
1 lb. crimini mushrooms
1 lb. shiitake mushrooms
½ cup pepperoncinis, chopped fine
½ cup onion, chopped fine
¼ cup red pepper, chopped fine
1 cup cider vinegar
½ cup water
¼ cup sugar
1 teaspoon garlic, minced
1 teaspoon juniper berries
1 tablespoon fresh tarragon, chopped
salt and pepper to taste

Remove stems from mushrooms and slice. In a stainless steel pan bring to a boil all ingredients except fiddleheads and mushrooms. Simmer for 15 minutes.

Add mushrooms and fiddleheads to the pan, bring back to a boil, and remove from heat. Refrigerate.

Serve on assorted greens for a light lunch or as an appetizer.

NOTE: Any assorted mushrooms may be substituted if those mentioned in the ingredients are not available.

Veal Oscar

1 lb. veal cutlets, pounded thin
16 asparagus spears, blanched
½ lb. king crab meat
milk as needed
2 eggs
flour seasoned with salt and pepper
bread crumbs
oil
butter

Place seasoned flour, eggs beaten with a little milk, and bread crumbs in three separate dishes. Dip veal cutlets first into flour, shaking off the excess, then into beaten eggs to coat thoroughly, then into bread crumbs. Press down to coat well and shake off excess. Heat oil and saute veal cutlets on both sides until golden brown. Keep warm in oven until needed.

Gently heat crab meat and asparagus in butter and arrange over veal. To serve, top with hollandaise sauce (recipe follows).

Hollandaise Sauce

4 egg yolks
2 sticks of butter, clarified
juice of one lemon
2 tablespoons white wine
Tabasco sauce, to taste

Place egg yolks and wine in a stainless steel bowl and whisk over a double boiler over medium heat until they are thick and lemon colored. Remove from heat and drizzle melted butter into the egg yolks, stirring until it is all absorbed. Stir in lemon juice and Tabasco to taste. Keep in a warm place until needed.

Salmon Athena

1 lb. salmon fillets, cut into 4 portions
phyllo leaves
½ cup Greek olives, pitted
1 lb. tomatoes, peeled, deseeded and chopped
2 tablespoons olive oil
8 oz. mushrooms
1 teaspoon garlic, minced
zest of ½ lemon
salt and white pepper to taste
1 stick butter, melted

Sauce ingredients:

1 cucumber, peeled, deseeded and chopped fine
1 cup yogurt
1 teaspoon fresh dill, chopped
2 tablespoons lemon juice
salt and pepper to taste

Combine all ingredients for sauce and refrigerate until needed. Heat oil, add minced garlic and saute for 30 seconds. Add tomatoes, mushrooms, lemon zest, olives and seasonings and saute gently for a few minutes until cooked through.

Place a phyllo leaf on a dry surface and brush with melted butter. Repeat this procedure with three more leaves, so you have four layered leaves, one on top of the other. Place a fillet of salmon in one corner of the phyllo and top with a few spoonfuls of the sauce. Roll up the phyllo dough in egg-roll fashion and brush with melted butter. Repeat with all four salmon fillets. Bake at 400 degrees for 20 minutes. Serve with sauce on the side.

Chocolate Marquise

This is a light creamy chocolate terrine served on a white chocolate custard sauce.

Terrine:
½ cup dried apricots, chopped
⅔ cup Armagnac, Cognac, or Cointreau
24 oz. bittersweet chocolate, chopped
1 cup butter, room temperature
1½ cups powdered sugar
10 eggs, separated
½ teaspoon cream of tartar

Combine apricots and liquor. Set aside to steep for 30 minutes. Melt chocolate over a double boiler, then cool until it is luke-warm. In a mixing bowl, beat butter and sugar until light and fluffy. Mix melted chocolate into the butter/sugar mixture by hand. Blend egg yolks into the chocolate mixture, one at a time, by hand. In a separate bowl beat egg whites with cream of tartar until they form soft peaks. Fold ⅓ of the egg whites into the chocolate mixture to lighten it, then fold in the rest of the egg whites. Pour this mixture into two small loaf pans lined with saran wrap and refrigerate overnight.

Sauce:
¼ cup butter, at room temperature
1 cup sugar
3 eggs
1 cup milk
1 teaspoon vanilla extract
8 oz. white chocolate, chopped fine

Beat butter and sugar in a mixing bowl until light and fluffy. Beat in eggs one at a time. In a small saucepan, bring milk and vanilla extract to a boil. Whisk hot milk into butter/egg mixture. Immediately whisk in chopped chocolate while sauce is hot. Continue to whisk until sauce is smooth. Let sauce cool and then refrigerate.

Serve two thin slices of chocolate terrine per person on a puddle of white chocolate custard sauce.

DOWN UNDER II

Down Under II is in a rambling clapboard building located beside the Masthead Marina overlooking Greenwich Bay in Warwick. The weathered-wood exterior of this spanking new contemporary restaurant blends in well with its surroundings and the picturesque harbor on Naragansett Bay's west side.

Some say Down Under II was so named because to get there you have to go down and under the Amtrak railroad line which skirts the shore. Supposedly, the Down Under restaurant in Fort Lauderdale, Florida was also inspirational in the naming of its Rhode Island counterpart.

Ken Gootkind, a former cooking instructor, and John Scanlon, a graduate of the Culinary Institute of Glasgow, Scotland, collaborated to start this seaside eatery in 1986. John runs the kitchen, and Ken does just about everything else. The partners also run City Lights, a trendy cafe in Davol Square, Providence.

The decor, although decidedly New England, with its clapboards and salty look, has shades of contemporary California or Florida. It's a bit of a paradox—elegant and classy to be sure, but chic and unassuming at the same time.

The spacious restaurant has seating for over 300, counting the upstairs and the outside. The main restaurant is on the ground floor, but there's an upstairs bar and lounge, called Moonlighting, with a separate menu. And outdoors, you can dine (in the summer) with a great view of the bay from the terrace or verandas. The upstairs is split-level, with an elevated bar made of African mahogany overlooking the lounge which opens to a veranda and the bay.

The interior is rustic by-the-sea New England combined with more than a touch of elegance. The ground-floor rooms are connected by French doors and provide an airy impression that's enhanced by the multi-paned colonial-style windows that line the wall. The aquamarine trim matches the napkins, but mostly everything else is white for nice contrast. Tiny unobtrusive spotlights and scallop shell wall lamps provide most of the lighting. The tables are far enough apart so personal intimacy is maintained. The impression of vastness, so common in other large restaurants, is mitigated by the separate rooms. So coziness is preserved.

As you might guess, Down Under II specializes in fresh seafood, mostly locally-caught. Sauces, fruits and garnishes are frequent accompaniments. For example, the Sole Jamaican is lightly floured, sauteed and served with kiwi fruit, banana and a lemon cream sauce. The chef's specialty is Bouillabaisse, made in the classical style with poached lobster, shrimp, clams and swordfish. At Down Under, they serve harpooned swordfish, which is immediately removed from the water and therefore more flavorful than the netted kind, which can become waterlogged. There's also a variety of steaks: the New York Sirloin Carpetbagger is stuffed with oysters, and the Cajun Sirloin is stuffed with Tasso, a spicy smoked ham.

The desserts are made on the premises and include "Death by Chocolate," a triple chocolate torte; a peanut-chocolate cheesecake; and a deep-dish marshmallow brownie. They also bake their own sweet cinnamon bread and whole-wheat bread sticks.

The wine list is highlighted by several good Australian bargains, California Chardonnays, French reds, twenty wines available by the glass, and house drafts.

During the summer, watch the sailboats ply the bay and enjoy cookouts on the terrace, accompanied by outdoor live entertainment. Overall, a romantic experience with a dash of sea salt.

DOWN UNDER II

A waterfront restaurant
One Masthead Drive, Warwick • (401) 885-6400

DINNER: 5:00 to 10:00, weekends until 11:00
SEPARATE BAR: Moonlighting
CHILDREN'S PORTIONS: not available
CREDIT CARDS: all major cards accepted
PARKING: ample free parking
RESERVATIONS: advised

Cajun Clams

48 littleneck clams, shucked, on the half-shell
1 cup red pepper, diced
1 cup green pepper, diced
1 large Spanish onion, sliced
1½ lb. andouille (Cajun sausage)
½ lb. butter
5 cloves garlic, minced
1 cup sliced pepperoncini
1 or 2 cups breadcrumbs
2 tablespoons cayenne pepper
2 tablespoons white pepper
2 tablespoons black pepper
1 tablespoon onion powder
1 tablespoon garlic powder
1½ tablespoons basil
1½ tablespoons oregano
½ tablespoon thyme
¼ tablespoon salt
2 tablespoons paprika

Saute together the red and green peppers, sliced onions, and andouille in butter until the vegetables are soft. Thoroughly mix in all other ingredients except the clams and breadcrumbs. Then mix in enough breadcrumbs to reach a desired consistency. Stuff the littlenecks with this mixture and bake at 350 degrees until browned. Finish with a little melted butter.

Clams Piri Piri

8 stalks celery, sliced on bias
1 large Spanish onion, sliced
1 cup diced red peppers
1 lb. chourico, sliced
1 cup pepperoncini, sliced
48 littleneck clams, scrubbed
2½ cups white wine
2 tablespoons tabasco
½ cup oil

Combine all ingredients (except clams and wine) in a large sauce pot and simmer at medium heat for approximately 25 minutes, stirring frequently. Then add clams and white wine. Steam, tightly covered, until clams open. Serve in large soup bowls.

Chicken Frangelico   SERVES 8

4 lbs. boneless chicken breast, skinned and cut into medallions
1½ cups Mandarin orange sections
1 cup toasted almonds
1½ cups flour
¼ lb. butter
8 oz. hazelnut liqueur
10 large eggs, beaten

Heat butter in a saute pan. Dredge chicken pieces in flour, shake off excess, and dip in beaten egg until well coated. Saute in hot butter for approximately 2 minutes; then turn over and cook for an additional 2½ minutes. Drain off butter and toss in orange sections and toasted almonds. Flambe with hazelnut liqueur and serve immediately.

Veal Mikeal   SERVES 8

2½ lbs. Provimi veal medallions
2 cups red grapes, peeled
6 roasted green peppers, quartered
2 cups flour
8 oz. Marsala
4 oz. demi-glaze
8 oz. butter

Melt butter in a saute pan. Dredge veal medallions in flour and add to hot butter in saute pan. Cook for 45 seconds to one minute before turning; cook for an additional 2½ minutes on other side. Drain off butter and add peeled red grapes and roasted green pepper quarters. Flambe with Marsala wine. Add demi-glaze and cook for 2 minutes. Serve immediately.

Bouillabaisse

8 jumbo shrimp, peeled and deveined
24 littleneck clams
1½ lbs. fresh bay scallops
1 lb. swordfish, cubed
1 lb. tuna steak, cubed
1 lb. monkfish, cubed
4 whole lobsters (tails and claws)

 Sauce:
1 bunch leeks, rinsed well and sliced on the bias
1½ lbs. diced tomatoes
2 cups white wine
1 cup orange juice
¼ tablespoon fennel
¼ tablespoon tarragon
¼ tablespoon basil
1 tablespoon sugar
½ gram saffron
2 cloves garlic, minced

Combine all ingredients for sauce in a large saucepot. Simmer on medium heat for one hour, stirring frequently. When sauce is done, add the fresh seafood and cook for 12 minutes, tightly covered, or until clams have opened. Serve with plenty of crusty French bread.

WATERFRONT · RESTAURANT

ARBORETUM RESTAURANT

Located in an unlikely East Providence neighborhood in the shadows of the Washington Bridge, the **Arboretum Restaurant** occupies the former home of the Industrial National Bank. The building is a restored classic Greek Revival structure built in 1920. For a while, the building also served as headquarters for the Rhode Island Lottery. The huge bank vault still remains and serves as a pantry.

The interior is reminiscent of an English club. Four magnificent brass chandeliers dominate the high ceiling, imbuing a soft glow over the room. The spacious interior is made surprisingly intimate by clever lighting and ingenious seating arrangements. The tables are placed far enough apart so privacy is assured. Brocaded banquettes serve as section dividers. The opulent scene is further enhanced by starched white linen, plush carpeting, burnished silver service, white china and a waitstaff all dressed up in snappy black and white uniforms. On the left, as you enter, there's a long cocktail bar where you can relax and listen to live jazz on Friday and Saturday nights.

Bob and Jill Jaffe took over the Arboretum in 1988 and, in collaboration with executive chef Paul Fraunfelter, began creating a new menu. The Continental dining format served their ambitions well—to provide food drawn from a variety of cultural influences ranging from traditional preparations to many new offerings that combine elegant flavorings with good nutrition, using lighter sauces and high quality ingredients. It is vital to the Jaffes that all patrons are provided with a fine dining experience, even those with dietary concerns or restrictions.

As a result, the Jaffes have created a diverse selection of ingenious and lively dishes such as Chicken Yucatan, a marinated boneless, skinless chicken breast topped with a chile mole sauce and served with a grilled jalapeno pepper on a bed of sauteed jicama (a Mexican vegetable). You may find jicama elsewhere, like on your salad. "We use it on salads because it tastes great raw or cooked; it's always crisp," explains Bob Jaffe.

The meatless entree consists of chick peas in a tangy tomato-based sauce served with grain and vegetables. The chef often uses grains like quinoa ("keenwa"), a high-protein alternative to rice imported from South America, or basmati rice, an aromatic long-grain rice imported from India.

The Steak Henry IV is a filet mignon grilled over hardwood coals and served with a mushroom cap, artichoke hearts and a rather unique Bearnaise sauce flavored with shallots and herbs. The crisp boneless duck comes with an inventive Indian tamarind sauce blended with spices, raisins and dates.

The creativity continues with the entree accompaniments, which might be potatoes cut in the shape of button mushrooms, or a medley of fresh vegetables, grilled or sauteed to enhance flavors and provide visual appeal. Vegetables with any dinner may be ordered steamed by request. Even the house salad is exciting—a potpourri of greens with radicchio, arugula, red lettuce and other seasonal greens. Choose your own homemade dressing.

The desserts include Satin Cheese Pie, a smooth cream cheese layer topped with a sour cream glaze. Maxmillian's, on Hope Street, supplies the ice cream truffles and fresh fruit sorbets, and a premium low-fat ice milk that you would swear is "high test." And the coffee beans, ground daily, are from The Coffee Exchange on Wickenden Street.

The wine list includes several "by the glass" specials and a house Yvon Blanc (white French Bordeaux).

The surroundings are undeniably elegant, but you'll feel comfortable and have no trouble enjoying yourself, whatever your mood.

ARBORETUM RESTAURANT
Fine dining in comfortable, elegant surroundings
39 Warren Avenue, East Providence • (401) 438-3686

LUNCH: 11:30 to 3:00, Mon. to Fri.
DINNER: 5:30 to 10:00, Mon. to Thurs., Fri. & Sat. 5:30 to 11:00
LATE SUPPER: until 11:00 Fri. and Sat.
SEATS: 80 — 100
CHILDREN'S PORTIONS: are available by request
CREDIT CARDS: AMEX, MC, VISA
PARKING: ample free parking in private lot
RESERVATIONS: advised

Pescatore
SERVES 2

2 tablespoons extra virgin olive oil
2 cloves garlic, minced
4 large shrimp, peeled and deveined
4 large or 8 to 12 small scallops
6 mussels, scrubbed and debearded
6 clams, scrubbed
2 tablespoons fresh parsley, minced
2 cups Italian plum tomatoes with juice
**   or fresh tomatoes, diced, skins removed**
½ teaspoon red pepper flakes
2 teaspoons fresh basil, minced
8 to 10 oz. linguine, cooked al dente

Heat olive oil in a large saute pan over medium high flame. Add garlic and cook until golden brown. Add seafood, cover and cook over high flame for 5 minutes. Add all remaining ingredients, except pasta, and bring to a boil. Add pasta and saute for 1 to 2 minutes until heated through. Serve in a warmed bowl, arranging seafood decoratively.

Grilled Tuna Steak with Sun-dried Tomato Vinaigrette SERVES 4

4 6-oz. tuna steaks

Marinade:
1 clove garlic, minced
1 teaspoon fresh basil, minced
1 tablespoon extra virgin olive oil
½ cup dry sherry

Vinaigrette:
1 cup sun-dried tomatoes (packed dry, not in oil)
2 tablespoons balsamic vinegar
10 Calamata olives, pitted (brine packed)
1 tablespoon parsley, minced
1 tablespoon garlic, minced
2 tablespoons lemon juice
2 tablespoons extra virgin oil
2 tablespoons white wine

Combine all the ingredients for the marinade and marinate the tuna steaks, turning occasionally, for one hour. Soak the sun-dried tomatoes in boiled water for 30 minutes, then drain. Puree all vinaigrette ingredients, including tomatoes, in a food processor.

Grill tuna steaks over hot coals until cooked but still juicy. Place on a warmed plate. Top each steak with one to two tablespoons of vinaigrette at room temperature and serve.

Refrigerate remaining vinaigrette for later use.

Arboretum

R E S T A U R A N T

Grilled Veal Tenderloins with Goat Cheese Pesto

3 lbs. whole veal tenderloins, peeled and cleaned
Marinade:
2 cloves garlic, minced
½ cup extra virgin olive oil
¼ cup lemon juice
1 tablespoon Dijon mustard
¼ cup balsamic vinegar
1 tablespoon parsley, minced

Pesto:
4 cloves garlic, minced
2 bunches fresh basil, trimmed and cleaned
   (about 4 cups loosely packed)
1 cup extra virgin olive oil
½ cup pine nuts
6 oz. chevre cheese

Combine all of the ingredients for the marinade in a large bowl. Add veal tenderloins and marinate for at least one hour.

In a food processor combine garlic and basil. While the machine is running, add the oil in a steady stream. Blend until smooth, scraping down the sides of the bowl when necessary. Add half of the pine nuts and the chevre. Blend for one more minute until all the ingredients are incorporated thoroughly. Reserve.

Grill tenderloins over hot coals until done. Place on a warmed serving platter. Spoon one tablespoon of the pesto over the center of each tenderloin. Garnish with remaining pine nuts and sprigs of parsley and serve.

Figs in Blankets

1 package filo pastry
1 package dried Calamata figs
1 cup sliced almonds
½ cup Amaretto
¼ cup honey

Almond Cream:
1 cup sliced almonds
1 tablespoon butter
¼ cup flour
1½ cups heavy cream
1 cup skim milk
¾ cup sugar
½ cup Amaretto

Strawberry Syrup:
2 pints strawberries, washed and hulled
1 cup strawberry liqueur
½ to ¾ cup sugar depending on taste

To make the fig pastries: Preheat oven to 350 degrees. Spread almonds on a baking sheet and toast in oven for about 10 minutes until golden brown.

Cut the hard ends off the figs and discard. Place the figs, almonds, Amaretto and honey in a food processor and run machine until all ingredients are combined to make a paste. Spread fig mixture along filo pastry in a thin line. Roll and cut to make a pastry about the size of a small cigar. Repeat until all the fig mixture is used.

Place pastries on an ungreased baking sheet and bake for 15 to 20 minutes or until golden brown. Let cool to room temperature.

To make the almond cream: Saute the almonds in the butter over medium high heat until golden brown. Sprinkle in the flour and stir until it absorbs all of the butter. Stir in the cream and skim milk, reduce heat to medium low, and heat through. Add the sugar and Amaretto and continue to heat until the sauce coats the back of the spoon. Remove from the heat and puree the mixture in a food processor or blender. Set aside and let cool to room temperature.

To make the strawberry syrup: Put the strawberries, strawberry liqueur and sugar in a saucepan over high heat and bring to a boil. Reduce heat and let cook for 20 minutes. Remove from heat and puree mixture in a food processor. Strain mixture through a sieve or cheesecloth to remove solids. Set aside and let cool to room temperature.

To assemble: Spread a bed of the almond cream evenly on a plate. Place two of the fig pastries on the cream, parallel to each other. Drizzle the strawberry syrup around the edges of the plate and, with a knife, pull the syrup through the cream to make swirled patterns.

NATHANIEL PORTER INN

The Nathaniel Porter Inn is a restored colonial mansion listed as "architecturally outstanding" on the National Register of Historic Places. You'll find the inn near the waterfront in the historic district of Warren, Rhode Island.

Owners Bob and Paulette Lynch rescued this colonial gem from certain destruction and have lovingly restored it to its former elegance. The building, a victim of fire and years of neglect, had been slated for demolition, which accounts for the symbolic phoenix rising from the ashes on the Nathaniel Porter sign outside.

The restoration process uncovered an astonishing treasure trove of architectural features: extraordinary hardwood floors (oak, mahogany and parquet), a venerable baking oven, early American stencilling (beneath countless layers of paint and wallpaper), and an 1810 French mural.

Nathaniel Porter himself was a Minute Man who, at the age of twelve, fired on the British at that famous battle of Lexington in 1775. Bob Lynch traces his ancestry back to Porter, and named the inn after him.

The Lynches opened the Nathaniel Porter Inn in 1986, after five years of restoration. When you discuss the restaurant business with this charming and unpretentious couple, you get the feeling that Bob is a man with a mission and Paulette is a canny administrator.

Their philosophy on the restaurant business can be seen throughout the inn. "Before we opened the inn, we made a list of all the things we didn't like about restaurants and set out to correct them, putting ourselves in the customer's place," Bob explains. "A customer shouldn't have to wait more than ten seconds before being greeted at the door, and that greeting must be warm, friendly and sincere. If customers with reservations have to wait more than fifteen minutes, we'll buy the drinks."

The bill of fare and the style are uncommon—elegant and romantic, but not pompous. The portions are hearty, served on large oval plates with pleasing visual presentation. It's a no-nonsense menu in which the sauces will enhance but not overpower.

You may have encountered microscopic lamb chops before, but you won't find them here. They serve two five-ounce chops, char-broiled, and finished off with a sauce of Pinot Noir wine, shallots, garlic, cranberries and a touch of black pepper. There's also a thick-cut filet steak flambeed in cognac with roasted hazelnuts and Dijon mustard.

Other popular entrees are Scallops en Croute (scallops in a puff pastry with lobster-mornay sauce) and the novel Oyster Fettucini, a combination of fresh spinach with a special cream sauce of onions, white wine, herbs and spices.

For a special colonial treat, try the Chicken with Mary Washington's Oyster Sauce. The boneless breast of chicken is filled with oysters and spinach and served with Mary's oyster sauce. It was one of her son's favorite (recipe follows).

The seafood steaks are a staple, and you may find salmon, swordfish or tuna. You'll get a large steak either char-broiled or served with an ocean sauce.

Imaginative appetizers include sauteed venison slices with a sauce of mushrooms, prunes and apricots; grilled shrimp in a strawberry-thyme sauce; or calamari sauteed in lemon butter and flamed with Drambuie.

Try one of the innovative salad dressings, like garlic-mustard (recipe follows), you won't find them anywhere else.

The dessert tray features Nathaniel Porter's famous Autumn Harvest Apple Pie, a delicious combination of sweet and tart apples enhanced with pumpkin and cranberries (recipe follows). *Yankee Magazine* judged this pie to be the best in Rhode Island.

The fare at the Nathaniel Porter Inn changes with the seasons, and the fall and winter are times for special celebrations. Yule Log Night (in mid-December), Thanksgiving and New Year's Eve are celebrated with traditional meals served before blazing open fires.

Flickering candlelight, cozy dining rooms and waitresses dressed in period linen-and-lace pinafores create an authentic setting for a romantic respite removed from the everyday. And if you are weary after all this food and conviviality, check with the innkeepers— the Nathaniel Porter Inn has several guest rooms upstairs.

NATHANIEL PORTER INN
Innovative Cuisine in a Traditional Country Inn
125 Water Street, Warren, Rhode Island • (401) 245-6622

OPEN: every day of the year, except Christmas Day & New Year's Day
LUNCH: 11:30—2:30
AFTERNOON TEA: 2—3
DINNER: 6 to 10:00 (may vary with season)
SEATS: 75
CREDIT CARDS: AMEX, DC, MC, VISA
PARKING: ample free parking in back
RESERVATIONS: advised

Lady Margaret Chicken
SERVES 4

4 8-oz. chicken breasts, slightly pounded
2 cups bread crumbs
2 cups egg wash (equal parts of water and beaten egg)
2 cups flour
2 tablespoons olive oil

Dip chicken in flour, then egg wash, then bread crumbs. Saute chicken breasts in an oven proof pan with 2 tablespoons olive oil. Brown on both sides. Transfer to an oven and cook for seven minutes at 350 degrees. Serve with Lady Margaret Sauce (recipe follows).

Lady Margaret Sauce
SERVES 4

¼ cup mushrooms, sliced
¼ cup carrots, diced
¼ cup scallions, sliced
¼ cup onions, sliced
1 tablespoon butter
4 tablespoons ketchup
2 tablespoons heavy cream
¼ teaspoon chili powder
½ cup white wine

Saute sliced vegetables in butter. When they are soft, deglaze the pan with wine. Add ketchup, cream and chili powder. Reduce sauce until thickened. Serve over Lady Margaret Chicken.

Grilled Stuffed Tuna Steaks   SERVES 4

4 1-inch thick tuna or swordfish steaks
½ teaspoon dried sage, rubbed
2 oz. mozzarella cheese, grated
salt and pepper to taste

Cut a deep pocket in each tuna steak by inserting a sharp knife in the side of each steak and carefully moving it back and forth to enlarge the pocket. Sprinkle salt and pepper over the fish. Toss the sage and grated cheese together in a bowl and stuff each fish steak with the cheese mixture. Grill over a charcoal fire until fish is opaque. Pour melted butter on top before serving.

Mary Washington Chicken   SERVES 4

4 8-oz. boneless chicken breasts, slightly pounded
fresh spinach leaves

Stuffing:
1 onion, thinly sliced
½ cup oysters, shucked
1 to 1¼ cups bread crumbs
3 tablespoons oil
½ cup white wine

Saute onions in oil until translucent. Add oysters and saute for one minute. Add wine, bring to a boil, and add bread crumbs to make a stuffing mix.

Lay each chicken breast out flat and cover with spinach leaves. Place a large spoonful of stuffing on one side of each chicken breast and roll up. Secure with toothpicks. Place each rolled breast in a microwavable dish and wrap with plastic. Place in a microwave oven and cook on high for 5 or 6 minutes. Serve with oyster sauce (see below).

Oyster Sauce   SERVES 4

½ cup oysters, shucked
1 onion, thinly sliced
1/8 teaspoon mace
1 teaspoon salt

½ teaspoon pepper
juice of one lemon
1 tablespoon butter
½ cup bread crumbs
½ cup white wine
heavy cream

Saute oysters and onion in butter until opaque. Season with mace, salt, pepper and lemon juice. Add wine and cook for one minute, remove from heat and mix in crumbs. Add heavy cream until smooth. Serve over Mary Washington Chicken.

Garlic-Mustard Salad Dressing

1 egg
⅓ cup Pommery mustard
⅔ cup red wine vinegar
2 tablespoons garlic, chopped
2 cups olive oil
salt and pepper to taste

Mix together egg, mustard, vinegar and garlic in a bowl. Whisk in oil until all ingredients are well combined. Season with salt and pepper and serve.

New England Tea Scones

4½ cups flour
1¼ teaspoons baking power
½ teaspoon baking soda
1 teaspoon cinnamon
½ teaspoon nutmeg
4 tablespoons sugar
pinch of salt
½ lb. butter
10 oz. raisins
2¼ to 2½ cups heavy cream

Combine flour with baking powder, baking soda, spices, sugar and salt. Cut butter into flour to make a coarse meal. Mix in raisins. Gradually blend in heavy cream until dough is moist to the touch, but not too wet. Drop spoonfuls of the mixture into greased muffin tins. Brush with egg that has been beaten with a little cream. Bake in oven at 350 degrees for 20 or 25 minutes until done and golden in color. Serve warm, sliced in half and spread with butter and strawberry preserves.

Autumn Harvest Apple Pie

Crust:
2 cups King Arthur flour
¾ cup butter
2 tablespoons Crisco shortening
½ cup sugar
pinch of salt
1 egg

Filling:
2 cups firm sliced apples
1 cup sliced soft apples
1½ cups fresh cranberries
1 cup fresh pumpkin (1 or 2 slices)
⅓ cup canned pumpkin
½ cup sugar
1 tablespoon lemon juice
1 teaspoon flour
½ teaspoon ground ginger
½ teaspoon cinnamon
¼ teaspoon ground cloves
¼ teaspoon allspice
3 tablespoons butter

In a bowl, combine flour, sugar and salt. Cut in butter to a fine meal. Add shortening and egg and mix to form a dough. Roll out dough and cut out two circles to form a pie crust.

Cut apples and pumpkin in thin slices into a large bowl. Combine all other ingredients, except butter, and mix into the apple mixture. Fill pie crust with apple mixture and dot the butter in pats over the filling. Top with pie crust. Brush top with egg wash and bake for one hour and 15 minutes at 350 degrees. Serve warm with slightly sweetened whipped cream or ice cream.

HEMENWAY'S

Charles Martin Hemenway (1886-1964) was an enthusiastic sportsman and keen businessman (president of Moxie Beverage Co., the New Haven Railroad, and Decca Records). In 1985 his grandson, Ned Grace, inspired by this spirit of excellence and entrepreneurship, decided to name his new restaurant **Hemenway's**. Charles Hemenway's favorite sport was fishing, and Hemenway's specializes in seafood.

Noticing a surprising shortage of fine seafood restaurants in Providence, Grace was on the lookout for the perfect spot. When a superb location became available in historic Old Stone Square, he took action and opened Hemenway's.

The restaurant's spacious interior is an interesting combination reflecting both historic and contemporary Providence. The atmosphere is decidedly open-air. The broad main room, with a thirty-foot high ceiling, is bordered on three sides by vast plate glass windows offering a panoramic view of revitalized downtown Providence. Elegant mahogany and brass adornments abound, including an enormous elevated bar with beveled glass insets and a custom-built wine cabinet which greets you at the door. There's also a fascinating wall-length mural depicting Old Stone Square at the turn of the century. Look for the nautical neon decorations tastefully stationed around the interior.

Hemenway's is a seafood extravaganza. They regularly fly in all sorts of fish and shellfish from around the world. You may find stone crab from Florida, Norwegian salmon, Dover sole, and all kinds of exotic Hawaiian varieties. The menu lists seventeen varieties of oysters, and although they're not all available at the same time, it indicates the scope of Hemenway's selection.

Everything is fresh, and it's a Herculean task to keep track of all the incoming seafood shipments. Hemenway's refrigerator truck is continually shuttling between Providence and Boston's Logan Airport to keep the restaurant supplied with fresh seafood.

A fresh menu is printed every day, so no need to squint at blackboard specials. The menu runs the seafood gamut. In addition to an extensive oyster bar, appetizers range from clams and mussels to squid, bluefish and trout. Typical entrees could include Boston scrod, Florida grouper or marlin, New Bedford haddock, Maryland soft-shell crabs, mako shark, pompano, swordfish, and of course, lobsters (from little chickens to four and five pounders). Hemenway's Clambake is a conglomeration of lobster, fish, mussels, steamers and assorted other goodies. They also serve seafood casseroles, chowders, salads and fried dinners. Okay, they have steaks and chicken, too.

You'll love the seafood so much, you'll want to take some home. Well, you can. There's a retail fish market right in the restaurant, but don't expect the usual odiferous corner fish market—this one's a spiffy little store with everything from Hemenway's menu. You can't miss the imposing lobster pool fashioned from New Hampshire granite, and look for a copy of the *Encyclopedia of Fish* behind the counter.

General manager Gerry Fernandez has an extensive culinary background, including his education at the renowned Johnson and Wales College of Culinary Arts. According to Gerry, "Hemenway's is Rhode Island's seafood address, and that's pretty good in the Ocean State."

HEMENWAY'S SEAFOOD GRILL & OYSTER BAR
"Our fish story is a tale of seafood dining at its finest"
One Old Stone Square, South Main Street, Providence • (401) 351-8570

LUNCH: 11:30 to 3:00, except Sundays
DINNER: 5:00 to 10:00, Fri. & Sat. 4:30 to 11:00, Sun. Noon to 10
LATE SUPPER: Fri. & Sat. 9:30 to 11:00
SEATS: 220
CHILDREN'S PORTIONS: are available
CREDIT CARDS: AMEX, CB, DC, MC, VISA
PARKING: free valet parking after 5 p.m. in the building
RESERVATIONS: advised for parties of 8 or more

Petro's Zesty Barbecue Sauce ONE PINT

1 pint Open Pit barbecue sauce
   (or your own favorite)
½ cup whole ripe tomatoes, diced fine, seeds and all
½ cup Bermuda onion, diced fine and sauteed in butter
4 dashes Tabasco sauce
1 teaspoon Cayenne pepper
1 tablespoon Chablis

Combine sauteed onions with chopped tomatoes and allow to cool. Combine all ingredients in a stainless steel bowl and refrigerate overnight.

This spicy sauce is excellent as a dipping sauce for any full-flavored fish, and goes very well with chicken wings too. For grilled or baked fish, spread the sauce thinly over the fillet and cook. Serve with an additional spoonful of sauce on the side.

Hemenway's Herb Butter YIELD: 1 lb.

1 lb. lightly salted butter
1 tablespoon fresh lemon juice
¼ teaspoon celery salt
¼ teaspoon Cayenne pepper
3 tablespoons fresh dill, chopped fine
3 tablespoons fresh chives, chopped fine
3 tablespoons fresh parsley, chopped fine
½ teaspoon Worcestershire Sauce
2 dashes Tabasco
½ teaspoon garlic powder

Soften butter to room temperature in a stainless steel bowl. Add remaining ingredients and blend well with a wire whip. Refrigerate for at least one hour to allow flavors to blend.

This butter can be used on any fresh or frozen fish. It's also good on baked or grilled shellfish such as lobster, crab, clams and oysters. Spread over fish fillet before cooking and dot the fish again with pats of herb butter before serving.

Tomato-Dill Mayonnaise

SERVES 2

1½ cups mayonnaise
¼ cups tomatoes, seeded and chopped
2½ tablespoons fresh dill, chopped
1 teaspoon fresh lemon juice
¼ teaspoon salt
2 or 3 turns black pepper

Combine all ingredients in a stainless steel bowl and blend well with a wire whip. Refrigerate for at least one hour to allow the flavors to blend.

This sauce can be used with most grilled fish, although oily fish is best. Spread mayonnaise liberally over the fish fillet and bake at 375 degrees or grill over a hot fire. It is also very good with smoked fish, or as a salad base.

Grilled Lobster Tails

SERVES 2

6 fresh North American lobster tails, uncooked
  (or frozen)
½ cup Hemenway's herb butter
1 teaspoon "Old Bay" brand seasoning
2 fresh dill sprigs
4 lemon wedges
1 cup rock salt

Split lobster tails (in the shell) lengthwise and brush meat side with melted herb butter. Sprinkle the tails lightly with "Old Bay" seasoning and place on a very hot grill, meat side down, for two mintues or until lightly browned. Turn the lobster tails over so that the shell side is directly on the grill, and brush the meat with herb butter. Serve on a plate lined with rock salt (to keep the shells level) and garnish with lemon and fresh dill sprigs. Serve immediately.

If North American lobster tails are not available, substitute with South American, Florida rock lobster, or South African rock lobster tails.

This grilling procedure also works very well with crab or shrimp. You may want to serve this grilled seafood with your favorite dipping sauce, such as cocktail sauce, or Chinese duck sauce.

Grilled Idaho Rainbow Trout SERVES 2

2 rainbow trout, whole boned fish
1 cup Petro's barbecue sauce
4 lemon wedges
2 parsley sprigs, chopped very fine

Open each whole boned fish and lay it flat, skin side down, on an oven pan that has been oiled. Brush the fillets with Petro's barbecue sauce and let stand for five minutes. Grill on high heat for 3 or 4 minutes on each side. Remove to serving platter immediately and lightly glaze fish with warmed barbecue sauce once more. Sprinkle with chopped parsley. Garnish with lemon wedges and parsley sprigs and serve.

Frozen fillets can also be used, but should be thawed overnight in the refrigerator. Petro's barbecue sauce is also excellent on grilled swordfish, white marlin, mako shark, and other full-flavored firm-fleshed fish. The fish can also be baked if you prefer.

Native Rhode Island Tautog SERVES 2

1½ lbs. tautog fillets
juice from one lemon
1 tablespoon white wine
4 tablespoons tomato-dill mayonnaise
2 fresh tomato slices
4 fresh dill sprigs
salt and white pepper to taste

Sprinkle fish fillets with lemon juice, white wine, salt and pepper and let stand for 10 minutes. Pat fillets dry with a clean towel and spread liberally with tomato-dill mayonnaise. Bake in a preheated oven at 375 degrees for 10 minutes or until the mayonnaise mixture is golden brown and the fish flakes. Garnish with a sprig of fresh dill and tomato slices that have been dusted with salt and pepper and then blackened, Cajun style, in a hot skillet with only a drop of oil or butter.

This recipe works very well with bluefish, salmon, or any other oily or firm-fleshed fish. The tomatoes can be dusted with your favorite Cajun spice before being blackened to add more zip.

RUE DE L'ESPOIR

Deborah Norman fulfilled a dream when she opened **Rue de l'Espoir** on a shoestring in 1976. The "Rue", as it's affectionately known, was Deb's first ownership venture in the restaurant business. After a brief career of odd jobs (cook, bartender, house painter), she scraped together the funds and set out as an entrepreneur. Rue de l'Espoir ("street of hope"), appropriately located on Hope Street, is now an East Side institution recognized as a cosmopolitan European bistro serving a diverse selection of food.

The exterior of this one-story (the upper floors burned years ago) 19th-century wood-framed building is decorated with green and white awnings and flower boxes. You'll pass through the stylish entrance hall amidst a variety of posters and enter the restaurant to your right (the bar is through the left door).

In the restaurant, the rough-cut wide-board floors and multitudinous hanging plants blend nicely with the dark blue and off-white woodwork. Original paintings of Paris street scenes, bistro lights (globes) and fresh flowers round out the ambiance. The broad multi-paned windows enhance the soft, cheery interior.

The bar has huge hanging plants, tile-topped tables and a high tin ceiling. There are pretty half curtains on the windows and French murals on the side wall depicting harlequin-like Paris street scenes. The hardwood floor and a neon "Rue" behind the bar complete the charming image.

In menu design and food preparation, Deborah Norman collaborates with chef Michael Koussa, a RISD School of Culinary Arts graduate and luncheon chef Glen Dona, a Johnson and Wales alumnus. "We continually review our menu to meet the ever-changing palates of our customers," explains Deb Norman. "America's newest food craze is grazing, and we offer a dozen small plate specials."

The small plates are an affordable way to sample a variety of fare. Try mushrooms stuffed with pesto and baked with parmesan cheese; tai crab cakes with cilantro and ginger; imported artichoke hearts stuffed with roasted red peppers, sun-dried tomato, fresh farmer's cheese with a plum tomato sauce; or home-smoked shrimp tempura. You can even mix and match with the Rue Rue Platter, a sampler of any five small plates.

Rue de l'Espoir participates in the movement toward good nutrition, and the main menu includes plenty of pasta, whole-grained oven pizzas and large salads.

Rue de l'Espoir is serious about pasta, and innovative too. You can choose from oven-baked penne (quill-shaped pasta) with sausage, zucchini and fontina cheese; Shangai shrimp bun tao (bean thread pasta) sauteed with pineapple, banana and coconut and served with a spicy peanut sauce; or Rasta Pasta (Jamaican) served with a spicy sauce and grilled chicken (see following recipe). For a different twist, try the goat cheese lasagna with spinach, mushrooms and sun-dried tomatoes.

The whole wheat pizzas are on the leading edge of modern cuisine. Choose toppings like pesto and roasted pine nuts; four cheeses with fresh tomato and rosemary; or shrimp, sun-dried tomato, green onion and mozzarella.

Salad specialists can live their fantasy at the Rue. The Salad Nicoise is an imaginative blend of the required tuna, egg and black (Calamata) olives supplemented with hearts of palm, marinated green beans and red new potatoes. The Mediterranean Salad is a medley of marinated eggplant, red and green peppers, zucchini, tomatoes, onions, chick peas and Calamata olives in olive oil, garlic, cumin and anisette. The Macadamia Nut-Raspberry Vinaigrette Salad is a who's who of leaf lettuce with mixed greens of red oak, red sail, peppercress, tatsoi, mizuna, mache, arugula and radicchio.

Rue de l'Espoir is well-known for complete dinner entrees, which vary nightly but could include jumbo shrimp stuffed with an oyster, brie and brioche pate; roasted grilled duck with caramelized onions and lingonberries (sauce recipe follows); or veal medallions sauteed with porcini mushrooms and Madeira demi-glace.

Rue de l'Espoir is a Providence culinary landmark that's obviously not satisfied to rest on its laurels.

RUE DE L'ESPOIR
Fine French cooking and elegant dining
99 Hope Street, Providence • (401) 751-8890

BRUNCH: Sun. 11:30 to 2:30
LUNCH: 11:30 to 2:30 Tues. to Sat. (closed Mon.)
        Closed for lunch Sat. and Sun. from early June through late August
DINNER: 5:00 to 10:00, Tues. to Sun. (closed Mon.)
LATE SUPPER: Fri. & Sat. until 11:00
SEATS: 75
CHILDREN'S PORTIONS: not available
CREDIT CARDS: all major credit cards accepted
PARKING: on street
RESERVATIONS: advised

Rasta Pasta Sauce with Grilled Chicken

SERVES 4-6

Sauce:
½ cup chicken stock
½ cup orange juice
1 teaspoon chili paste
2 teaspoons sesame oil
2 teaspoons oyster sauce
2 teaspoons honey
2 teaspoons tamari
1 teaspoon garlic, chopped
1 teaspoon ginger, minced
⅓ cup sherry
1 cup cornstarch thickener

1 green pepper, minced
1 red pepper, minced
1 onion, minced

Combine all ingredients for sauce in a pan and bring to a boil. Thicken with a cup of cornstarch thickener.

Saute peppers and minced onion in olive oil until onions are transparent. Add sauce to onions and peppers and heat through. Toss in fettucine, and top with pieces of grilled chicken. Garnish with sliced bananas.

Grilled Asparagus, Red Pepper, Cashew & Dill Pesto

SERVES 4-6

3 asparagus spears, grilled and cut into small pieces
¼ can roasted red peppers
½ cup roasted cashews
⅓ cup fresh dill
⅓ cup fresh basil
1 cup butter, melted
1 cup olive oil
3 tablespoons minced garlic
salt, pepper and nutmeg to taste

Place all ingredients in the container of a food processor and mix until well blended. Season to taste with salt, pepper and nutmeg and toss with hot pasta of your choice.

Filet of Sole Meuniere

SERVES 4-6

2 lbs. filet of sole
1 cup clarified butter
½ cup lemon juice
½ cup rum (light or dark)
6 bananas, sliced
¾ lb. roasted almonds, chopped
2 cups seasoned flour for dredging

Heat a little clarified butter in a saute pan until butter is hot. Dip dried fish filets in flour, shake off excess, and saute for about two minutes in hot butter on each side. Place fish filets on a warm serving plate as they are cooked. Add lemon juice, rum, sliced bananas and roasted almonds to the pan and deglaze. Pour sauce over fish and serve immediately.

Macadamia Basil Pesto
Potato Salad
SERVES 4-6

1½ lbs. new potatoes, boiled, quartered and chilled
Pesto:
½ cup roasted Macadamia nuts
½ cup parmesan cheese
1 cup olive oil
½ cup fresh basil
2 teaspoons garlic
½ cup balsamic vinegar
⅓ cup Dijon mustard
salt, pepper and nutmeg to taste

Place all ingredients for pesto in a food processor and mix until they are well blended and nuts are chopped.

Place quartered, chilled potatoes in a bowl and toss well with pesto. Season to taste with salt, pepper and nutmeg and serve.

Orange Lingonberry Caramelized
Onion Cassis Sauce
SERVES 4-6

1 or 2 jars lingonberry preserves
1 onion, sliced
2 tablespoons butter
⅓ cup cranberry juice
⅓ cup orange juice
⅓ cup Cassis
½ teaspoon each salt, pepper, nutmeg and ground
    ginger

Place all ingredients in a sauce pan and bring to a boil. Simmer for 10 minutes. Thicken with ½ cup cornstarch and water and simmer for another 10 minutes. Serve over roasted grilled duck.

Thai Crab Cakes

SERVES 4-6

1 lb. snow crab meat
⅓ cup cilantro
⅓ cup celery, chopped
½ cup onion, chopped
¾ cup egg whites
¼ cup corn meal
¼ cup flour
1 teaspoon chili paste
1 teaspoon ginger
salt, pepper and nutmeg to taste

Saute celery and onion in butter until translucent. Add all other ingredients and mix until well blended. Form into pancakes 4 inches in diameter and saute in olive oil until golden on outside. Serve with Lime Creme Fraiche (recipe follows).

Lime Creme Fraiche

2 cups sour cream
½ cup heavy cream
½ cup fresh lime juice
2 teaspoons salt

Place all ingredients in a mixing bowl and beat until well blended. Keep at room temperature for at least six hours before serving. Serve with Thai Crab Cakes.

IN PROV

In Prov is a popular watering hole and eatery located in a dramatic setting in the main lobby of the ultra-modern Fleet Center overlooking downtown Providence's Kennedy Plaza. Business people, theater-goers and tourists have made In Prov a favorite for breakfast, lunch, happy hour, dinner and after-dinner. The In Prov can be many things to many people, but no one will find it dull.

The decor is decidedly contemporary and urbane. The stylish split-level interior with its striking plate-glass windows offers an expansive view of bustling Kennedy Square. Plate glass also forms a long interior wall, stretching to the ceiling of the main lobby and opening onto an indoor patio cafe in the arcade. The restaurant is not large, but the high ceiling, indirect lighting and plate glass provide a spacious impression. The tiny dark-wood bar serves as an elegant focal point to take in the ambiance. Throughout the restaurant, you'll find an imaginative medley of textures and forms: tapestry cushions, Burgundy leather chairs, hand-sewn rattan chairs and stools, marble-topped iron cafe tables, and a profusion of glass and dark woods. Interestingly, various sections of the restaurant have different decors, but all are variations on the same contemporary theme. All of this was good enough to impress the judges at *Restaurant Business* magazine who awarded In Prov first prize for interior design.

John Elkhay and Guy Abelson opened In Prov in 1985 after spending a year designing the concept and another year in construction. Both John and Guy have extensive experience in the restaurant business. After cooking for several years at various New York City restaurants, John became head chef at the famed Jared Coffin House on Nantucket. Later, he worked as executive chef with Guy at Cafe in the Barn, before the two opened In Prov. Guy also owns Cafe in the Barn, a charming restaurant located in Seekonk, Massachusetts.

John, who holds a Guinness record for making the most omelets in thirty minutes (315), needs his high energy level to carry out the demanding duties of managing partner and head chef at In Prov. "We want In Prov to be a fun place to dine and enjoy wine," says John. "Our menu is casual but elegant, and we serve all our wines (over 30) by the glass. We want our customers to feel at ease wearing either a tuxedo or jeans."

In addition to its diverse selection of wines, In Prov offers a unique menu and is well known for its Tapas—a Spanish tradition of serving a variety of small portions, allowing customers to sample many dishes at one meal.

The food is cooked in an open-air kitchen, mostly on a rotisserie or a mesquite grill. The culinary influences are varied—Southwestern, French, Chinese—and there's something to appeal to all palates. The menu, changing four to six times a year, is roughly seasonal. The most popular Tapas are the Duck Tostada, a grilled duck breast with sauteed vegetables, peanut sauce and jicama orange salad; and the Southwestern Grilled Chicken Breast, served with salsa, sour cream and grilled vegetables on a flour tortilla.

The rest of the Tapas run the culinary gamut, and you may find chive angel hair pasta with veal, prosciutto and crunchy vegetables in a garlic-cream sauce; Bento Box Sampler, a Japanese-style assortment of grilled shrimp, seared peppered tenderloin, tempura vegetables and sweet-and-sour cucumber noodles (each sample is served in a separate compartment of the box); or Lo Mein Yu Hung Lo, a stir-fry of swordfish, broccoli, mushrooms, snow peas and peppers (a prize winner in the 1988 Providence Pasta Challenge). Other notable Tapas are fried crayfish tails with lime aioli; and Massachusetts goat cheese with chopped herbs, extra virgin olive oil, fruit and foccacia.

In Prov also serves regular entrees like Veal Paillard—grilled with a sauce of andouille sausage, veal bacon, grilled onions and mushrooms; or scallops sauteed with julienne vegetables, served with a Rhode Island Sakonnet Chardonnay cream sauce on puff pastry.

For dessert, try the Pinon Nut Cake, a flour-less chocolate cake with passion fruit cream and three fruit sauces (apple, peach and blackberry). There's also a chocolate espresso mousse, and you can even get a banana split (with grilled bananas).

In addition to numerous wines, the bar boasts an extensive portfolio of liquor, beer and alcohol-free drinks. House drinks are all top shelf, and you can get all sorts of cognacs, armagnacs, brandies, liqueurs and rare sherries. Unusual specialty drinks are regularly available and might include a raspberry vodka gimlet or a rootbeer float with triple vanilla *gelato*.

In Prov also has an extensive gourmet take-out section with a separate menu offering an interesting selection of salads, sandwiches and soups.

Visit the In Prov and you'll get the impression that this chic establishment is right in tune with Providence's new sense of self-confidence and leadership.

IN PROV

Tapas and fine wines in a contemporary setting
50 Kennedy Plaza, Providence • (401) 351-8770

TAKE-OUT BREAKFAST: 7:30 to 11:30, weekdays only
LUNCH: 11:30 to 3:00, weekdays only
DINNER: 5:30 to 12:00
LATE SUPPER: Fri. & Sat. until 1:00 a.m.
BAR: 11:30 a.m. to 1:00 a.m., 2:00 a.m. on weekends
SEATS: 88
CHILDREN'S PORTIONS: not available
CREDIT CARDS: AMEX, MC, VISA
PARKING: valet parking at night; parking garage open during the day
RESERVATIONS: advised

Rhode Island Duck Tostada   SERVES 4

4 boneless breasts of Rhode Island ducks, marinated (recipe follows)
stir-fried vegetable filling (recipe follows)
6 tablespoons ripe olives, sliced
1 Boston lettuce, chiffonnade
1 medium-sized ripe tomato, chopped
4 blue corn tortillas
peanut sauce (recipe follows)

Marinate the duck breasts for at least 2 hours, preferably overnight. In the meantime, prepare the vegetable filling, sauce and grill.

Start your grill 30 minutes before dinner. We recommend using mesquite or any aromatic wood or hardwood charcoal. When the coals are evenly hot, grill the ducks skin-side down for approximately 6-8 minutes depending on the size of the breasts. Turn the breasts over and grill the other side until medium rare or rare.

Add 6—8 oz. peanut sauce to the stir-fried vegetables. Toss to incorporate the sauce. In ¼ inch of oil, fry the tortillas until crisp on both sides. Drain well on paper towels. Fill the tortillas with chopped lettuce, tomato and olives. Spoon the stir-fried vegetables with peanut sauce over the lettuce. Arrange the thinly sliced grilled duck on top. Serve immediately.

Duck Marinade

8 oz. soy sauce
2 dry chili peppers
2 tablespoons coriander leaves, chopped
2 tablespoons sesame oil
8 oz. sake
3 oz. orange juice
2 tablespoons honey
6 oz. water
3 teaspoons garlic, chopped
3 teaspoons ginger, chopped

Combine all ingredients and marinate the ducks in a stainless steel or ceramic bowl. Cover and let stand for at least 2 hours or overnight.

Peanut Sauce

1 cup soy sauce
4 tablespoons Oloroso sherry
3 teaspoons ginger, chopped
3 teaspoons scallions, chopped
3 cloves garlic, chopped
1½ cups chunky peanut butter
½ cup sesame oil
1½ cups extra virgin olive oil

Place all ingredients in a bowl or food processor and blend until smooth.

Stir-Fried Vegetable Filling

5-6 shiitake mushrooms, sliced
2 cups cabbage, shredded
½ red pepper, julienne
½ yellow pepper, julienne
1 carrot, julienne
½ head of radicchio lettuce, shredded
extra virgin olive oil as needed

In a very hot pan, stir-fry all the above ingredients for 4-5 minutes. Add salt and pepper to taste.

Santa Fe Spiced Shrimp with Blue Corn Cakes and Posole SERVES 2-4

16 large shrimp, peeled and deveined
8 oz. Ranchbier (smoked beer)
3 oz. Worcestershire sauce
4 oz. concentrated beef stock

Marinade:
1 teaspoon cayenne pepper
1 teaspoon chili powder
½ teaspoon rosemary, chopped fine
1 bay leaf, crushed
½ teaspoon granulated garlic
½ teaspoon dried oregano
½ teaspoon black pepper
½ teaspoon salt
¼ cup extra virgin olive oil

Mix all dry ingredients for marinade and combine with olive oil. Marinate shrimp for at least two hours, preferably overnight.

Heat a cast iron or stainless steel pan until very hot. Remove shrimp from marinade, place in pan and sear on all sides. Deglaze pan with 8 ounces Ranchbier or any good Mexican beer. Season with Worcestershire sauce and add 4 ounces of concentrated beef stock. Reduce to a sauce. Place hot blue corn cakes (recipe follows) on a plate and top with shrimp. Pour sauce over shrimp and decorate with Posole (recipe follows) and red pepper strips.

Blue Corn Cakes

2 cups water
1 oz. butter
salt
¾ cup blue cornmeal

Bring water to a boil and add butter and salt. Stir in cornmeal and cook for 3-5 minutes. Pour polenta into a greased cookie pan and spread evenly to ½ inch thick. Chill for several hours. Cut into desired shapes (circles or triangles) and grill or saute to reheat.

Posole

1 cup posole (southwestern dried corn kernels)
2 oz. double smoked bacon, chopped fine
½ onion, chopped fine
1 teaspoon white peppercorns
1 bay leaf
½ jalapeno pepper, sliced
chicken stock as needed, approximately 4 cups
salt and pepper to taste

Saute bacon. Add onion and seasoning. Add posole and cover with approximately 4 cups of chicken stock. Simmer for three or four hours until tender. Replace stock as necessary. Cool and store.

Grilled Lobster Ravioli
with Sakonnet Cream Sauce   SERVES 4

1 lb. fresh bay scallops
1 large brown egg
¼ cup heavy cream
½ teaspoon cayenne pepper
1 tablespoon fresh herbs, i.e., tarragon, thyme, chopped

1 teaspoon salt
1 teaspoon freshly ground black pepper
2 1¼-lb. lobsters
grilling spice
Sakonnet cream sauce (recipe follows)

In a food processor, puree scallops, eggs, heavy cream, cayenne pepper, herbs, salt and pepper. Transfer to a bowl and chill. Split the lobster tails lengthwise. Brush with extra-virgin olive oil and grilling spice. Grill the lobster over hot mesquite charcoal or aromatic hardwood charcoal until it is two-thirds done. Do not overcook the lobsters. Grill the claws with the top side on the grill so that the lobster fluid does not drain out. Remove the meat from the shell. Chop the meat into ¼ inch chunks and chill.

Combine puree and lobster meat. Set aside. Take a ravioli sheet and cut in half. Brush the bottom sheet with beaten egg. Place the lobster filling on the ravioli sheets in mounds. Place the top sheet and press down gently. Be sure to get the air out from around the filling and check to make sure the edges are sealed. Cut with a pasta cutter to form the raviolis.

Boil salted water in a large pot. Add raviolis and cook until tender. Place raviolis on a platter and spoon Sakonnet cream sauce over them. Garnish with chopped red pepper and chives.

Sakonnet Cream Sauce

8 ounces Sakonnet Chardonnay
16 oz. heavy cream
2-3 oz. concentrated chicken stock
4 oz. unsalted butter cut in 8 slices
1 teaspoon thyme, chopped
1 teaspoon tarragon, chopped
salt and pepper to taste

In a saucepan, reduce Chardonnay by two-thirds. Add cream. Heat and reduce mixture by one-third. Add chicken glaze and season with salt and pepper. Add thyme and tarragon. Remove from heat. Whip butter into sauce one piece at a time to create emulsion.

LA FRANCE

La France is the creation of June and David Gaudet, two former French teachers who got into the restaurant business by accident. As June tells it, "In 1979, we helped some French friends set up a restaurant in Narragansett, but soon they got discouraged and went home, and guess what? We're in the restaurant business!" Before long, the Gaudets had given up their teaching jobs and were working full-time in the restaurant business.

In 1982, they opened La France on Providence's East Side. Later they sold the Narragansett restaurant to focus soley on Providence, a more stable location than the seasonal seashore.

Both June and David have spent lots of time in France working and learning and are well-versed in French culture.

La France is in a humble building that disguises a plush interior patterned after a formal French country house. The Gaudets have lovingly and personally decorated this one-story building in exquisite style. You'll find deep red tapestried walls with fleur de lys bordering an original tin ceiling dating back to 1910. Note the gleaming brass fireplace fender above the dining room door, an unusual touch. The French ambiance is pervasive, but at the same time mellow and romantic. When you step inside La France, you step into an Old World fantasy.

La France specializes in traditional French recipes, the classics, rather than the more trendy modern cuisine, with an emphasis on special sauces that enhance and complement the carefully-chosen ingredients. The Gaudets shop at small local purveyors. "David shops daily, and personally inspects everything", explains June. "So everything is fresh and just the way we want it."

The menu is adjusted seasonally, but always features an interesting assortment of seafood, chicken, duck and beef. Portions are hearty and served with perfectly prepared fresh vegetables. You may find steak tartare with the traditional trimmings; roast duck smothered with cabbage, onions and apples with Reisling wine; or grilled salmon steak with Sauce Choron.

An interesting La France twist is serving veal the way other restaurants usually serve beef, like chateaubriand or filet mignon. The Chateaubriand de Veau is a whole tenderloin of veal beautifully attired and served with a subtle mustard hollandaise.

For an appetizer, try the artichoke vinaigrette served with garlic mayonnaise or the handmade French garlic sausage, grilled and served with a mustard mayonnaise.

The special dessert is Chocolate Decadence, a flour-less, dense French cake. It's rich and solid — near fudge — and topped with whipped cream and raspberries. Another popular dessert is Strawberry Dacquoise, a cake of meringue layers made with ground almonds and layered with fresh strawberries and whipped cream.

The wine list (mostly French and Californian) accommodates a broad range of types and prices. George Debeouf is the house wine.

Rhode Island radio personality Sherm Strickhouser, a regular La France patron, often selects the Caesar Salad, Steak au Poivre (a house specialty served with a pungent black peppercorn, garlic and cream sauce), and Bananas Forestiere (flamed in rum and garnished with pecans and vanilla ice cream).

LA FRANCE

Classic French & Continental Cuisine
960 HOPE STREET, PROVIDENCE • (401) 331-9233

LUNCH: Tues.-Fri. 11:30-2:30
DINNER: Tues.-Thurs. 5:50-9:30, Fri. & Sat. until 10
CLOSED: Sun. and Mon.
CREDIT CARDS: major credit cards accepted
PARKING: park on street
RESERVATIONS: recommended

Artichokes Vinaigrette

6 whole artichokes
2 tablespoons fennel seed
6 cloves garlic
1 orange, quartered
1 cup white wine
1 cup cider vinegar
1 tablespoon salt
1 teaspoon pepper

Cut the stems off the artichokes evenly, so they will stand up. Trim points from the leaf tips with scissors. Place artichokes in a single layer in a large saucepan. Add the fennel seed, garlic, orange, white wine, vinegar, and enough water to cover the artichokes.

Cover the pan and cook until the artichokes are tender. Cooking time depends on their size; generally about 30 to 40 minutes. Do not overcook or they will fall apart; they are cooked when a leaf can be easily pulled away and the meat comes off the leaves with the teeth. Remove artichokes when cooked and set liquid aside to cool. When the liquid has reached room temperature, put the artichokes back in the liquid and refrigerate.

To serve: Remove artichokes from liquid and drain upside down for a couple of minutes (give each one a gentle squeeze). Place each one upright on a serving plate with a dipping sauce of your choice: at La France we serve them with Aioli (recipe follows).

Aioli (Garlic Mayonnaise)

6 eggs
4 large garlic cloves, pressed
2 tablespoons lemon juice
2 generous tablespoons prepared dark spicy mustard
olive oil
1 teaspoon tumeric (for color, if desired)

Blend together eggs, garlic, lemon juice and mustard in a food processor until well mixed. With processor still running, pour olive oil into mixture in a VERY SLOW, STEADY STREAM until it becomes a desired mayonnaise consistency. Add tumeric to finished mayonnaise to color if so desired.

Steak au Poivre La France

8 steaks: strip sirloin, Delmonico, T-bone or
  porterhouse
3½ oz. black peppercorns, whole
48 oz. dry red wine (Rhone is best)
10 bay leaves
¼ oz. tarragon, dried (½ cup)
1 oz. fresh garlic, pureed (2 tablespoons)
1 tablespoon white pepper
2½ oz. beef stock
2½ oz. roux blond (see recipe)*
28 oz. heavy cream

Crush whole peppercorns in a blender for 30 seconds. DO NOT GRIND. In a heavy sauce pot, combine wine, bay leaves, tarragon, garlic, white pepper, crushed peppercorns and beef stock. Stir thoroughly and bring to a slow boil. Continue cooking, stirring occasionally, until mixture is reduced by half (approximately 30 minutes). When mixture is reduced, remove bay leaves with tongs.

Over low heat whisk in roux until mixture has the consistency of a thick porridge. (Add roux in teaspoon-quantities rather than all at once. Whisk roux in thoroughly.) Build sauce by slowly adding the cream, whisking the mixture constantly. The sauce is finished when completely blended. Remove to a bain marie or keep warm for at least an hour. (Sauce flavors peak after 24 hours, but can be used when just completed.)

Grill or broil steak to just below desired temperature. Place on a pre-heated hot sizzle platter. Ladle sauce over the steak, letting the sauce fill in the platter. Garnish as desired and serve immediately while the pepper-perfumed steam rises from the platter.

Roux Blond*

4 oz. butter
4 oz. all-purpose flour

Melt butter in a small saute pan. Add the flour and thoroughly blend. Allow mixture to just start to bubble over heat. Remove from heat and store at room temperature until needed.

Roast Duck a l'Orange

SERVES 2

one 4½ to 5 lb. roasting duck
1 or 2 oranges, quartered
salt and pepper to taste
2 tablespoons Cointreau

Sauce:

6 oz. can frozen concentrated orange juice
½ cup drippings from roasted duck
2 oz. Cointreau
zest from one orange

Preheat oven to 325 degrees. Pierce sides of duck with a fork so fat can drain while duck is roasting. Salt and pepper duck inside and out. Fill cavity with quartered oranges and brush duck skin with Cointreau. Place duck on a rack and roast until it is tender, approximately two hours, basting every 20 minutes with drippings and Cointreau.

Sauce: combine all ingredients in a heavy-bottomed saucepan and bring to a rolling boil. Reduce heat and simmer until zest is tender and sauce is thoroughly blended, about 20 minutes. Skim off any fat and pour over quartered, roasted duck and serve.

Strawberry Dacquoise

SERVES AT LEAST 10

1 quart strawberries
1 pint or more whipped cream

Meringue Layers:
2½ cups ground almonds
1½ cups sugar
8 egg whites
½ teaspoon cream of tartar
pinch of salt

Mix sugar and almonds together. Beat egg whites, cream of tartar and salt together until egg whites are very stiff. Fold sugar and almonds into the egg whites. Grease and flour two large sheet pans, or you may prefer to line the pans with grease-proof paper and lightly coat with oil. Draw two circles 10'' in diameter on each sheet pan or paper. Spread meringue mixture thickly on these circles to make cake layers. Bake in a slow oven at 275 to 300 degrees for about 40 minutes or until meringues are crusty on top. Cool layers thoroughly before attempting to remove them from the sheet pans. Using a long flat knife very carefully loosen and remove the meringue layers; or, if you have lined your pans with paper, peel off the paper.

To assemble the cake, cut strawberries in quarters and reserve some whole for garnishing. Fold the quartered strawberries into the whipped cream. Spread berry/cream mixture between the two layers of meringue. Coat the dacquoise with whipped cream mixture as you would frost a cake. Garnish the top with whole strawberries and serve in slices.

Chocolate Decadence Cake   SERVES 16

---

18 oz. unsalted butter
9 large eggs
1 cup strong coffee, preferably espresso
18 oz. chocolate
2¼ cups sugar
½ cup raspberry jam
2 tablespoons brandy or cognac
¼ cup whipped heavy cream
handful fresh or frozen raspberries

Line a 10" spring form pan with tinfoil. Lightly but thoroughly butter the lined pan. Whisk the eggs thoroughly and set aside.

Blend butter, coffee, chocolate and sugar in the top of a double boiler to melt. Heat gently to 130 degrees or until sugar dissolves and the chocolate melts; take care not to overheat. Remove from heat and whisk in eggs thoroughly. Pour into buttered pan and bake at 250 degrees for two hours or until center of cake is set. Completely cool cake on wire rack and refrigerate overnight. Serve chilled with warm raspberry sauce: heat ½ cup raspberry jam and 2 tablespoons brandy or cognac over low heat until the mixture is smooth. Add whole fresh or frozen raspberries. To serve: spoon a puddle of sauce on a serving plate, place a slice of chocolate cake on the sauce, and garnish with whipped cream rosettes.

RAPHAEL'S

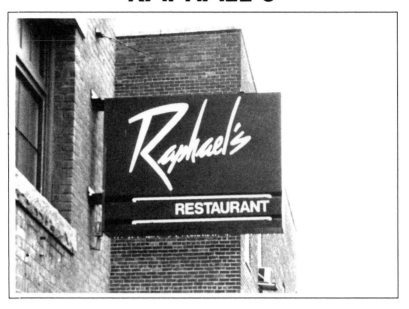

When you first walk into **Raphael's** you know this is not a garden-variety Italian restaurant. Raphael's is an imaginative combination of the old and new world.

Raphael Conte, the owner and chef, honed his culinary skills during a two-year stint in Italy, mostly in the Tuscany region. Raphael's mentor was his Italian uncle, a culinary professor. The philosophy Raphael gleaned from this experience is intimately intertwined in the heart and soul of the restaurant and nicely supplements his Johnson and Wales training.

The restaurant, opened in 1983, is housed in a superbly renovated turn-of-the-century mill from Providence's industrial hey-day. Raphael's airy interior is a pleasing mixture of the antique (huge exposed beams, a profusion of brickwork, ceiling pipes) and the modern (polished oak, contemporary furniture and salmon-hued walls).

The setting may lean toward the modern, but the style is strictly old world Italian. Raphael's specializes in regional Italian dishes, from Sicily to Milan. Everything is cooked to order; you won't find any steam tables here. Freshness is key.

The menu is biased towards health consciousness, not in a trendy *nouveau* style but in the traditional Italian way, with fresh pasta, veal, seafood and a diverse array of vegetables. As Raphael points out, ''The Italians eat mostly pasta, vegetables and seafood, and very little red meat.

But these are also the healthiest foods."

Appetizers include quail, calamari, prosciutto and littlenecks, all embellished and enhanced by tasty sauces, herbs and dressings. Main courses are dominated by pasta and seafood, as well as innovative house specialties. You may find grilled squid with hot cherry peppers in balsamic vinegar sauce, or a veal chop stuffed with veal sausage, spinach, pine nuts, mozzarella cheese and fresh tomatoes (recipe follows). Possibly the most imaginative dishes are the pasta/seafood combinations, in which the pasta and sauces are a perfect complement to fresh seafood like swordfish or sole. Raphael's is famous for its Crostini (recipe follows) — sliced country bread rubbed with olive oil and garlic and baked with slices of fresh tomato, mozzarella cheese and fresh basil. The wine list is mostly Italian with a few California wines. Pinero, a Pinot Noir, is the most popular.

The service, in the Italian style, is highly professional and attentive to detail. Don't be surprised when your napkin is refolded or your plates cleared promptly.

Raphael's is a family affair; Raphael's father tends bar and his mother is the manager.

Raphael's is a popular watering hole for the business and professional set after work. There's a separate lounge with frequent entertainment, often live jazz. In the summertime, you can dance under the stars and enjoy grilled pizza in the spacious brick courtyard.

Raphael's is contemporary and relaxing, not stuffy or formal. You don't need a jacket and tie, but these would not be out of place, either.

RAPHAEL'S

Regional Italian cuisine in a contemporary setting
207 Pine Street, Providence • (401) 421-4646

LUNCH: 11:30 on, Mon. through Fri.
DINNER: until 11:00 p.m.
LOUNGE: Piano Room open until 1:00 or 2:00 a.m.
COURTYARD: outdoor dining in June, July and August
CLOSED: Sunday
SEATS: 50
CHILDREN'S PORTIONS: are available
CREDIT CARDS: AMEX, MC, VISA
PARKING: free valet parking in private lot
RESERVATIONS: advised on weekends

Tri-Color Salad with Gorgonzola

6 leaves arugula
6 leaves radicchio
6 leaves Belgian endive
3 tablespoons extra-virgin olive oil
1 clove garlic, finely minced
½ cup Gorgonzola cheese, crumbled
1 cup heavy cream
juice of one lemon
salt and pepper to taste
dash Worcestershire sauce and Tabasco to taste

Heat garlic in oil. Add crumbled cheese and stir. Add heavy cream and reduce. Stir in fresh lemon juice and remaining ingredients. Season to taste with salt and freshly ground black pepper. Pour over salad greens and serve.

Crostini

2 slices day-old Italian bread
4 sliced tomatoes, preferably home-grown
2 slices fresh mozzarella cheese
2 fresh basil leaves, chopped
salt and pepper to taste
1 clove garlic, halved
2 tablespoons extra-virgin olive oil

Rub bread with garlic clove and olive oil. Place tomato slices on bread and top with mozzarella cheese. Sprinkle with basil leaves and season with salt and pepper. Bake at 375 degrees for about 10 minutes or until golden-brown and crispy.

Linguine with Broccoli Rabe   SERVES 1

¼ lb. linguini
2 cups broccoli rabe, cleaned and blanched
¼ cup extra-virgin olive oil
2 cloves garlic, finely minced
pinch crushed red pepper
salt to taste

Cook pasta in boiling water for eight minutes, or until al dente. Drain. Heat olive oil, add garlic and saute until lightly browned. Add rabe and cook for two more minutes. Add a pinch of red pepper and season with salt. Toss with pasta and serve with grated Romano cheese.

Stuffed Veal Chop

1 veal chop, butterflied
½ cup fresh spinach, chopped
½ cup veal sausage, chopped
2 tablespoons fresh tomatoes, chopped
2 tablespoons fresh mozzarella cheese, chopped
1 clove garlic, finely minced
3 tablespoons breadcrumbs
2 tablespoons olive oil
1 tablespoon pine nuts
¼ cup veal demi-glaze,
      or you may substitute brown sauce

Coarsely chop the spinach, veal sausage, tomatoes and mozzarella cheese. Place in a bowl and add garlic, breadcrumbs, oil and pine nuts. Combine mixture well to form a stuffing. Slit veal chop and stuff with stuffing. Bake at 375 degrees for twenty minutes. Serve with veal demi-glaze, or a brown sauce.

J. WALES SEAFOOD RESTAURANT

J. Wales is a spiffy, spanking-new practicum facility for Johnson and Wales University. The restaurant is located in Warwick, near T.F. Green Airport in a beautiful nautical-design building. The exterior lines of the dark-green and white building make it look like a ship; in fact, it may remind you of an ocean cruise, as you walk up the canvas-lined gangway and notice the thick opaque glass in the entrance portico—it's the pressure-resistant kind used underwater, and helps set the theme.

King Neptune seems to rule at J. Wales, and this feeling is pervasive, from the decor to the menu. The contemporary interior is light, bright and airy, with blond wood and soft pastels of pink and blue. Round skylights appear like portholes in the ceiling, and tiny track lights with curling black cords look like eels as they extend from the ceiling to shine on nautical lithographs dotting the walls. The bar, located in the center of the restaurant, is somewhat reminiscent of *20,000 Leagues Under the Sea;* it seems like a control room with tiny pink neon lights glowing vividly in the base of the bar. Hanging plants decorate the interior, and glass walls engraved with a wave motif serve as room dividers.

The menu is a cornucopia of seafood. However, landlubbers can order beef, chicken and veal dishes, as well as combination platters (seafood with either beef, veal or chicken). Pasta dishes are also numerous, particularly in combination with seafood.

Several house specialties headline the main menu (which reports the daily tides and weather) and include Fettuccine Galilee (named for the Rhode Island fishing port)—with scallops, clams and shrimp in a herb cream sauce (recipe follows); Seafood Lasagna—layers of fresh pasta with scallops, shrimp and cheeses with a rich tomato sauce; and Fillet of Sole Block Island—dipped in cornmeal and fried or baked. Daily specials always include a broad variety of seafood, and you might find catfish saute with lobster sauce, batter-dipped sole with pesto, baked trout with pinenuts, or broiled salmon with hollandaise.

As you might guess, J. Wales is deeply committed to lobsters. They serve them boiled, broiled or baked-stuffed, in various sizes. Choose yours from the lobster tank, if you wish.

J. Wales also serves a "Spa Cuisine" consisting of healthful dishes that are lighter but appetizing, like steamed salmon with fresh vegetables (recipe follows). Salads are served family style, with a creamy-dill house dressing, so you can customize your portion.

The vast menu of appetizers lists several Rhode Island specialties such as Narragansett stuffed quahogs, fried smelts, steamers and Oysters Apponaug (sauteed with capers and thyme). J. Wales' clam chowders are renowned and include both Rhode Island (broth with a touch of tomato) and New England (creamy). The fritters are famous too; they call them Warwick fritters, and you can get clam, corn or shrimp.

The wine list consists mostly of moderately priced American, French and Italian wines. The keying of entrees to suggested wines, listed by cellar number, is a helpful touch.

Ask your server to explain the Johnson and Wales program. The practicum students spend three months at J. Wales, and are supervised by teaching assistants (fellows) and the professional culinary staff. The students and fellows are engaging and spirited, with lots of enthusiasm for Johnson and Wales. All tips go into the student scholarship fund.

Before you leave, check out J. Wales Locker, a mini seafood stand where you can buy items from the menu to take home.

If you've never been on a cruise, J. Wales may be the next best thing.

J. WALES SEAFOOD RESTAURANT

*A seafood restaurant serving as a practicum facility for
Johnson & Wales culinary arts students*
2099 Post Road, Warwick • (401) 732-3663; SEA-FOOD

LUNCH: 11:30 to 4:30
DINNER: 4:30 to 10:00
LATE SUPPER: Fri. & Sat. until 11:00
SEATS: 180
CHILDREN'S PORTIONS: are available
CREDIT CARDS: AMEX, CB, DC, MC, VISA
PARKING: ample free parking
RESERVATIONS: advised, call SEA-FOOD

Fettuccine Galilee

SERVES 2

1 ounce oil
14 ounces fettuccine, blanched
4 ounces sea scallops, sliced if they are very large
8 each medium shrimp
8 each little neck clams
12 ounces heavy cream
4 each scallion greens, sliced
1 tablespoon tomato, peeled, seeded and diced
1 teaspoon basil, chopped
2 teaspoons parmesan, grated
1 teaspoon shallots, chopped
½ teaspoon garlic, chopped
Salt and white pepper to taste
½ ounce brandy

In a large, heavy saute pan, heat oil and add scallops and shrimp. Saute briefly and add shallots, garlic and brandy. Add cream and reduce until a sauce consistency is achieved. In a separate covered pot, steam open the clams in a little water. Keep clams warm until needed. When cream has thickened, add basil, salt, pepper, scallions and tomatoes. Add pasta and stir until pasta is hot and coated with sauce. Transfer mixture to two heated plates and ring with the cooked clams. Sprinkle with parmesan cheese and serve.

Steamed Salmon with
Fresh Vegetables Spa Cuisine SERVES 4

1 ¾ pounds salmon fillet
8 ounces white wine and water mix (equal parts)
1 large head broccoli
1 small red pepper
1 small green pepper
1 teaspoon fresh basil, chopped

Cut salmon fillet into equal portions. Cut broccoli into flowerettes, slice tender part of stem and add to flowerettes. Remove seeds and membrane from peppers and slice into fine julienne. Add to broccoli. Place water and wine in the bottom of a Chinese steamer. Place salmon fillets in one rack of steamer and place over liquid. Put vegetables and basil in another steamer rack and place on top of rack containing the salmon. Place steamer top on and turn flame to high. Steam until the salmon is just cooked (about 10 minutes). Place salmon on heated plates and arrange vegetables around. Garnish with lemon slices.

Sauteed Skate Wing
with Lobster Sauce SERVES 2

1 pound skate wing fillet
Flour to dredge fillet
1 ounce oil
Salt and white pepper to taste
6 ounces Buerre Blanc (white butter sauce)
3 ounces lobster meat, chopped

Have your fish dealer order about 2 pounds of skate wing and ask him to fillet it for you. Discard bones and skin. Heat oil in a heavy saute pan. Lightly flour skate fillet and saute in hot oil (about 2 minutes per side). Sprinkle with salt and pepper. Make buerre blanc sauce from any standard recipe and add chopped lobster meat to it. When skate is done, place on plate and top with lobster sauce. Serve with lemon and your choice of vegetable and starch.

Chocolate Truffle Cake

SERVES 12-14

1 pound semi-sweet chocolate (imported is preferred)
4 ounces olive oil
½ quart heavy cream, whipped
1 slice chocolate sponge cake, ¼ inch thick
½ ounce Grand Marnier or Triple Sec

Melt chocolate and oil together in a stainless steel bowl. Fold whipped cream into chocolate until mixture is smooth. Place mixture into a 8 or 9 inch round cake pan. Smooth out mixture and place a slice of chocolate sponge cake on top. Sprinkle sponge cake with Grand Marnier or Triple Sec and refrigerate for at least two hours.

Unmold cake in a hot water bath and place on a serving plate. Smooth top and sides with a knife. Sprinkle with a good quality cocoa powder. Cut cake with a hot, wet knife. Serve with whipped cream or creme fraiche.

ANGELS

Jaime D'Oliveira loves angels; he's collected them for years. So he had no trouble naming his new restaurant. The obvious choice was **Angels**. Angel icons are whimsically posted in different forms throughout the restaurant.

Angels conjures up images of Victorian Providence during its 19th century heyday. Housed in an antique building in the oldest part of Providence, Angels sits at the foot of College Hill in the shadow of Brown University and the Rhode Island School of Design. The long, narrow interior, with its unpretentious and understated ambiance is reminiscent of an earlier, simpler time.

When Jaime D'Oliveira opened Angels in the fall of 1988, he was fulfilling a life-long dream. After sixteen years in the restaurant business, being everything from head chef to dishwasher, he was ready to make his move. So when a prime location in an historic Providence building became available, he jumped at the opportunity.

Culinary art is deeply ingrained in Jaime's psyche. He learned cooking from his parents; his French mother and Portuguese father were both skilled kitchen practitioners. "My father had an outdoor grill that he used all year, you could see the footsteps in the snow", says Jaime.

You'll enter through a haloed portico, into a cozy dining room dominated on one side by a classic bar. Mirrors behind the bar and on the opposite wall give a spacious impression making the room seem larger than it actually is. The narrow room has an abundance of dark wood which contrasts nicely with the white table linen and lace curtains. The Victorian image is further enhanced by paisley wallpaper, ceiling lamps, overhead fans and marble columns.

There's an air of conviviality about Angels which attracts a diverse clientele looking for relaxation and style. The bar, where full dinners are served, is the focus of this activity.

You may glimpse the snappy white-coated chefs through the window of the tiny kitchen that efficiently turns out an amazing array of carefully prepared dishes without the benefit of either microwave or freezer. "In the European style, we go shopping every morning. First we pick up our bread at Palmieri's on Federal hill, next we visit local food shops to see what's special, and then we go back to Angels where the creative process begins", explains Jaime.

Much of the food is wood-grilled, but the grilling is not just reserved for the entrees, many of the vegetables as well as the ingredients in the soups and sauces are first grilled over the wood. Instead of pungent mesquite wood, Angels uses a more subtle hardwood charcoal, although there may be supplements of either apple, cherry or birch wood, to convey a more distinctive flavor.

Angels' menu is consistent with a growing movement back to simple food, the food known as "the kind mother used to make." Large porterhouse or Delmonico steaks are common. But the steaks aren't smothered with exotic sauces (instead look for house ketchup). Wax beans and mashed potatoes are likely accompaniments. The mashed potatoes, made rich and creamy with skins included, are appropriately called "Heart Attack Potatoes". Also, don't be surprised to find house applesauce and macaroni and cheese along with your pork chops. Sauces are not abundant but, when served, are normally found beside the entree and not covering it.

Although there's a pleasing simplicity about many of the dishes on the menu, they are, at the same time, unique and inspired. Portuguese, Italian and French influences are strong. You might find Portuguese Cioppino, a medley of clams, mussels, squid and chourico (Portuguese sausage); grilled chicken breast accompanied by orange honey butter, a sweet potato biscuit and grilled winter root vegetables (squash, onions and turnips); or grilled pork tenderloin with a spicy fennel stuffing and a fig port sauce.

Appetizers might include grilled tuna with green onions, radicchio and cannelini beans or tomato ravioli filled with lobster in a pink cream sauce.

Not surprisingly, the dessert menu includes angel food cake (with toasted coconut, hot fudge and whipped cream). Also, look for country-style blueberry cobbler served with heavy cream, and Viennese chocolate cake served with a raspberry sauce.

The wine list includes Italian, French, American and German wines. There are house wines, usually a Cabernet Savignon and a Chardonnay.

Angels also serves lots of wines by the glass, using a nitro-tap system to ensure freshness. The bar holds an extensive selection of ports and cognacs.

While Jaime is intimately involved in every aspect of Angels' operation, he relies heavily on his small, skillful staff to run the business smoothly. The team approach is clearly evident and there's no tension in the air. Like the clientele, they seem to be having fun.

ANGELS
Intimate dining in a Victorian atmosphere
125 North Main Street, Providence • (401) 273-0310

DINNER: 5:30 to 11:00 (closed Sun.)
BAR: until 12:00, 1:00 Fri. & Sat. (closed Sun.)
SEATS: 50, including the bar
CREDIT CARDS: AMEX, MC, VISA
PARKING: park on street
RESERVATIONS: not taken

Grilled Chicory Salad   SERVES 4

---

2 heads Belgian endive
2 heads radicchio
2 heads frisee or 1 large head chicory
½ cup extra-virgin olive oil
3 tablespoons sherry wine vinegar
½ cup raw pistachio nuts, chopped

Prepare grill. Light a charcoal fire and allow 35 to 45 minutes for the fire to reach the right temperature. Coals should be glowing red hot under a light grey ash.

To make the dressing, whisk together the oil and vinegar with approximately ½ teaspoon salt and freshly ground black pepper to taste.

Slice radicchio and Belgian endive in half vertically. If using frisee, prepare as above. If using chicory, divide the head into four equal parts. Brush chicory with olive oil. Place endive on hot grill. After two minutes, place radicchio on the grill. After another two minutes, place frisee or chicory on the grill. This last green will cook quite quickly. Turn chicory for even grilling as necessary. Chicory should retain some of its original texture.

Arrange one of each type of chicory attractively on each plate. Brush with the dressing and then drizzle more dressing around the plate. Sprinkle with pistachio nuts and garnish with lemon wedges.

Grilled Salmon with Garlic Cream and Tomato Butter

SERVES 4

4 fillets of salmon, 6 oz. each
salt and white pepper to taste
4 basil leaves for garnish

Tomato Butter:
2 large tomatoes, quartered
1 clove garlic
1 branch basil leaves
2 sprigs parsley
2 shallots, sliced
½ small carrot, cooked
1 cup dry white wine
2 tablespoons very good sherry or
    red wine vinegar
6 oz. unsalted butter, softened

Garlic Cream:
1 medium-sized baking potato, peeled and sliced
6 large garlic cloves, peeled and thinly sliced
approx. ½ cup milk
approx. ½ cup heavy cream
salt to taste

To prepare tomato butter: puree tomatoes, garlic, basil leaves, parsley, one shallot and carrot and reserve. Chop remaining shallot and place in a large saucepan with the white wine and vinegar. Reduce over medium heat until one tablespoon remains. Pour in reserved tomato puree and cook over medium heat until it is thick. Reduce more if necessary (most of the liquid should evaporate, making the flavor intense). Whisk in butter, a little at a time, over low heat. Strain into a clean saucepan and season with salt and pepper. Add more vinegar if necessary. Keep warm.

   To prepare the garlic cream, cook potato and garlic in milk and cream (equal amounts to cover) until potato is tender. Puree in a food processor and strain mixture into a pan. Thin with cream if necessary. Add salt to taste.

   Season both sides of salmon fillets with salt and pepper. Grill for three or four minutes each side over a hot grill, or until just cooked. Spoon garlic cream into the center of each plate and surround with tomato butter. Top garlic cream with a salmon fillet and garnish with a basil leaf.

Angels' Spoonbread Souffle
SERVES 6-8

2 cups light cream, scalded
1 cup milk
1¼ cups Gray's yellow cornmeal
6 tablespoons butter
1½ teaspoons salt
8 eggs, separated
1 small red pepper, diced
1 small orange pepper, diced
2 jalapeno peppers, chopped fine

Preheat oven to 375 degrees. Lightly butter a 1½ quart baking dish. In a large mixing bowl, combine dry ingredients. Add milk, stirring until smooth. Scald cream in a heavy saucepan and stir in butter. Add cornmeal mixture gradually, stirring until smooth. Cook over medium heat, stirring constantly until mixture begins to boil. Remove from heat and stir in egg yolks one at a time. Beat egg whites until stiff but not dry. Stir a quarter of the egg whites into cornmeal mixture, then fold in remaining egg whites. Spoon gently into a prepared baking dish. Bake for 30 or 45 minutes or until spoonbread is a puffy golden brown. Serve immediately.

Macadamia Nut Tart with Coconut Ice Cream
SERVES 8

Tart Crust:
¾ lb. flour
3 oz. sugar
½ lb. unsalted butter, cut into small cubes
2 egg yolks
2 tablespoons heavy cream

Place flour, butter and sugar in a Kitchenaid type electric mixer with hook utensil (or with regular beater if hook is not available). Mix until mixture resembles coarse cornmeal. In a small bowl, beat egg yolks and cream together. Gradually add egg mixture to flour mixture. As soon as it is blended, turn off mixer. Use immediately, or store in refrigerator wrapped in plastic wrap.

Roll out crust to ¼" thick and line a 12" tart pan. Bake at 400 degrees until just under golden brown.

Macadamia Filling:
½ cup unsweetened coconut
1½ cups raw macadamia nuts
6 tablespoons unsalted butter
1½ tablespoons honey
3 tablespoons heavy cream
3 egg yolks
¼ cup brown sugar
3" piece of vanilla pod

Toast coconut at 325 degrees until light golden brown. Toast nuts until they smell "nutty" and are slightly browned. Split vanilla pod and scrape out beans with a paring knife.

Place butter, honey, vanilla beans and pod in a small saucepan. Boil! You are making a brown butter—the butter will turn golden brown and you will smell a nutty aroma. Remove from stove and stir in cream. Combine with egg yolks and sugar just until thoroughly mixed.

Chop the nuts and stir them and the coconut into the sugar mixture. Pour into pre-baked tart shell and bake at 375 degrees until set and golden brown (about 20 minutes). Serve tart warm with whipped cream, ice cream (see following recipe), and fresh pineapple cut into chunks.

Coconut Ice Cream   SERVES 6-8

2½ cups shredded coconut
2½ cups milk
1½ cups heavy cream
6 egg yolks
3" piece vanilla pod

Toast coconut in oven at 325 degrees until golden brown. Split vanilla pod and scrape out beans. Place pod, beans, milk and toasted coconut in a non-corroding saucepan. Heat to just under a boil and let steep at that temperature for 20 or 30 minutes. Strain mixture and measure to be sure you still have 1½ cups of liquid left. If not, add milk to make up 1½ cups.

Whisk egg yolks in a bowl until just combined. Whisk in hot coconut milk. Pour mixture into a clean saucepan and return to the stove. Heat over a moderate flame, stirring constantly with a rubber spatula. Be sure to scrape bottom and sides of pan while stirring. Mixture will thicken quickly. When custard coats the back of a spoon, remove the pan from the stove and strain liquid into a clean bowl. Whisk in heavy cream. Chill custard and freeze according to the instructions of your ice cream maker. Ice cream should chill for 24 hours before serving. Serve with Macadamia Nut Tart.

PASTICHE

When you're in the mood for dessert and coffee, go up to Federal Hill and try **Pastiche**, a unique dessert cafe overlooking Providence. Pastiche is the brainchild of Brandt Heckert and Eileen Collins, two native Rhode Islanders who have no formal background in the pastry arts, but enjoy the challenge of running a bakery.

Brandt and Eileen started on a small scale baking for restaurants in their home. However, they soon moved the growing business to an outside location. Later, encouraged by customers' suggestions, they began gradually directing the business toward the dessert cafe it is today.

Pastiche is located in a restored 100-year old building with a commanding view of Providence from atop historic Federal Hill. Textured wall paper and decorative columns impart a kind of Mediterranean look to the interior. Pastel hues, light-wood tables, hardwood floors, indirect lighting, beautifully done window boxes, a working fireplace and potted plants complete the charming picture.

Pastiche (as its name suggests) produces a medley of delicious tortes, tarts and cakes. The desserts, profusely displayed in several glass cases, include a Chocolate Truffle Torte—a smooth flour-less torte combining puree of chestnut with rich chocolate; Lemon Mousse Cake—alternating layers of chiffon sponge and lemon mousse covered in a lemon buttercream; and Chocolate Orange Bavarian Torte—walnut sponge cake filled with dark-chocolate ganache and orange Bavarian cream, finished with orange buttercream. Also, Pastiche is renowned for its rich and creamy chocolate mousse cake and its various fresh fruit tarts—seasonal fruits in an all-butter tart shell filled with vanilla custard (recipe follows).

Desserts are available by the slice or as either small cakes (serving eight to ten) or large cakes (serving fifteen to twenty-five). Also, the pastry staff will make cakes for special occasions like birthdays or weddings.

Pastiche serves cappuccino, espresso and a variety of gourmet coffees. Try the house blend; it's an imaginative combination of Sumatran and Columbian French Roast coffees. The cafe also serves several refreshing non-alcoholic drinks.

The Old World style of Pastiche blends well with the atmosphere of Federal Hill. You'll find this little cafe a relaxing treat.

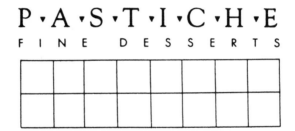

PASTICHE

Fine desserts and coffee
92 Spruce Street, Providence • (401) 861-5190

OPEN: 10 a.m. to 6 p.m.
CLOSED: Sun. and Mon.
CREDIT CARDS: not accepted
PARKING: free parking available
RESERVATIONS: not necessary

Apple Coffee Cake

5 oz. almond paste
½ cup sugar
8 oz. unsalted butter
4 whole eggs
1⅓ cups all-purpose flour
1⅓ teaspoon baking powder
1 teaspoon lemon rind
4 extra-large apples, sliced thick

Cream almond paste, butter and sugar until fluffy. Add eggs one at a time. Add dry ingredients and lemon rind. Pour batter into a paper-lined, greased and floured spring form pan. Arrange apples in a circular design on top. Sprinkle the top with ¼ cup granulated sugar and ½ teaspoon cinnamon. Bake in a preheated oven at 350 degrees for approximately 35 to 40 minutes, or until a cake tester comes out clean. Let cake cool at room temperature.

This cake may be glazed with ½ cup apricot jam mixed with ½ cup water and simmered for 3 or 4 minutes. The glaze must be very hot and completely smooth.

Blueberry Sour Cream Tart

Filling:

2 egg yolks
1½ cups sugar
1 lb. sour cream
1 teaspoon vanilla
2 pints fresh blueberries, washed and drained

Mix together sugar, sour cream and egg yolks with a whisk in that order. Add vanilla and set aside.

Tart shell:

8 tablespoons unsalted butter, cut into small pieces
1 teaspoon orange rind, grated
1 cup all-purpose flour

2 tablespoons sugar
½ teaspoon salt
5 tablespoons warm water
11" tart pan or quiche pan

Mix together warm water and salt and refrigerate. Mix dry ingredients, add butter, and grind in food processor until mixture resembles coarse meal. Pour into a large bowl and add chilled salt water and orange rind. Mix until it forms a dough. Flatten into a circle and refrigerate overnight. Take out 20 minutes before rolling.

Freeze the unbaked tart shell for 20 or 30 minutes before baking. Bake with a foil lining and weights at 350 degrees for 20 minutes. Remove foil and bake for another 5 minutes. The shell should be golden brown.

To assemble tart: Mix drained blueberries with the sour cream/custard mixture and pour into the pre-baked tart shell. Bake this mixture at 350 degrees for approximately 25 to 35 minutes. It should be set when cooked, but not brown. Let tart cool at room temperature and then refrigerate for about 3 or 4 hours before serving.

INDEX

BOOK ORDER FORM

Quantity	Title	Amount
_____	**A TASTE OF PROVIDENCE** @ $7.50	_____
_____	**A TASTE OF NEWPORT** @ $7.50	_____
_____	**A TASTE OF CAPE COD** @ $7.50	_____
_____	**A TASTE OF PROVINCETOWN** @ $6.50	_____
_____	**THE BARONS OF NEWPORT** @ $7.50	_____
_____	**THE COMPLETE GUIDE TO NEWPORT** @ $5.95	_____
_____	**TRADITIONAL PORTUGUESE RECIPES FROM PROVINCETOWN** @ $6.50	_____
	TOTAL:	_____
	R.I. Residents add 6% Sales Tax	_____
	Shipping	_____
	TOTAL AMOUNT:	_____

Please add $2.00 for each book and $1.25 for each additional book for handling and shipping. For orders of two or more books, please give street adress so we can ship UPS.

Make check payable to:

PINEAPPLE PUBLICATIONS and mail to:
24 Bridge Street, Newport, R. I. 02840
(401) 847-0859